The Maya
The Story of a People

by Njord Kane

The Maya: The Story of a People.
By Njord Kane

© 2016 by Njord Kane. All rights reserved.

No part of this book may be reproduced in any written, electronic, recording, or photocopying form without written permission of the author, Njord Kane, or the publisher, Spangenhelm Publishing. You must not circulate this book in any format.

Books may be purchased by contacting the publisher and author at: spangenhelm.com

Published on: November 1, 2016 by Spangenhelm Publishing

Interior Design and Cover by: Njord Kane

Library of Congress Control Number: 2015939914

ISBN-13: 978-1-943066-032

ISBN-10: 1943066035

1. Maya 2. Mayan 3. History 4. Mesoamerica

Second Edition.

10 9 8 7 6 5 4 3 2

Spangenhelm Publishing
United States

Table of Contents

Preface.................page 1

Part 1
The Beginnings of a People

Chapter 1 - Who were the Maya?..page 1

Chapter 2 - The Paleo-Indian Period (First People - 3500 BC)....page 15

Chapter 3 - The Archaic Period (3500 BC - 2000 BC).....................page 33

Chapter 4 - The Preclassic Period (2600 BC - 200 AD)..................page 41

Chapter 5 - Early Preclassic (2600 BC - 1000 BC)...........................page 51

Chapter 6 - Middle Preclassic (1000 BC - 400 BC).........................page 61

Chapter 7 - Late Preclassic (400 BC - 200 AD)................................page 73

Chapter 8 - The Classic Period (200 AD – 900 AD).......................page 79

Chapter 9 - The Post-classic Period (900 AD – 1697 AD)............page 101

Chapter 10 - The Spanish Conquest of the Maya.......................page 113

Part 2
Ancient Maya Ways

Chapter 11 - The Maya Calendars .... page 135
    The Long Count .... page 141
    The Tzolkin .... page 147
    The Haab' .... page 151
    The Wayeb .... page 155

Chapter 12 - Ancient Maya Arithmetic .... page 159
    The Value of Zero .... page 169
    The Four Slave Example .... page 175
    The Grid System .... page 179
    Subtraction .... page 190
    The Finger Method .... page 195
    The Maya Abacus .... page 207
    Maya Concept of Fractions .... page 223

Chapter 13 - The Maya Codices .... page 229
    The Paris Codex .... page 232
    The Madrid Codex .... page 236
    The Dresden Codex .... page 240

Chapter 14 - The Maya Religion .... page 245
    Offerings and Sacrifices .... page 249

Chapter 15 - Maya Mythology .... page 253
    The Legend of the Hero Twins .... page 257

The Early Life of the Hero Twins.....................................page 263
The Defeat of Seven Macaw...page 265
The Sons of Seven Macaw..page 268
Discovery of One Hunahpa's Gaming Equipment.......page 273
The Xibalban Ballgames...page 276
Downfall of Xibalba...page 280
Death and Ascension of Hunahpu and Xbalanque......page 283

Chapter 16 - Maya Society..page 287
Houses...page 298
body modifications..page 301
Sacred Colors..page 310

Chapter 17 - Maya Weapons and Warfare...............................page 317

References...page 331

Preface

This book is divided into two parts. The first part tells the Maya story chronologically from an anthropologist's point of view. Starting from the "First Peoples" that migrated into the Americas as hunter-gathers (the Paleo-Indians) following herds of megafauna, such as Mammoth. Into the gradual progression of settling and forming into a complex society. Part two of this book, highlights specifics about ancient Maya culture, inventions, beliefs and practices.

The Maya were a major indigenous pre-Columbian civilization of the Yucatan Peninsula and are members of a modern American Indian people of southern Mexico, Guatemala, and parts of Honduras who are the descendants of this ancient civilization.[199] Which is correct to use when referring to these people, is it 'Maya' or is it 'Mayans?' Is it a 'Maya' or a 'Mayan' archeological site? We see the words, Maya and Mayan used interchangeably without discrimination. So, which is correct, do we use Maya or Mayas or Mayan or Mayans?

The adjective 'Mayan' is used in reference to the language or languages, whereas the noun "Maya"[**mah-yuh**][199] is used when referring to the people, places, and or culture, etc., without distinction between singular or plural. This convention is the most widespread among Mayanists (scholars who study and write about the Maya). This distinction arose in the field of linguistics, where the "Mayan" adjective started to be used to define the linguistic family that incorporates the different dialects spoken by the Maya people. In sum, "Mayan" are their languages and "Maya" for everything else in reference.

The purpose of this book is to provide a concise and up to date historical chronicle about the Maya. With so many recent discoveries by archeologists studying the Maya and their ruins, many things that we had previously knew of the Maya civilization have changed. This makes the Maya story as previously taught out of date and needing to be retold. This book tells the Maya story current to Today's discoveries, presented in short chapters to maintain the reader's enthusiasm through each epoch of Maya history.

We start our story about the Maya from first existence as an identifiable and distinct people that had migrated into the Americans many thousands of years ago. We will bring you to their progression from hunter-gathers into agricultural settlements that grew into city-states. A journey through the rise and decline of the Maya civilization. Highlighting new discoveries in simplified Maya mathematics and technologies, that were previously a mystery to scientists, such as the resilient 'Maya Blue.'

This book is not the single work of the author, but the combined works of hundreds of years of thousands of researchers spending lifetimes trying to unravel the mystery of the Maya. There has been so many recent discoveries by modern researchers, the Maya story has almost been rewritten from what we thought we used to know about their obscure history.

Part 1

The Beginnings of a People

Chapter 1

Who were the Maya?

The Maya are an indigenous people whose culture had built a thriving ancient city-state civilization in Mesoamerica.

MesoAmerica is the location that lies in the area from Mexico to South America. An area considered to be the 'middle' of the Americas and is also known as the Central Americas.

Along with the Maya, there are many other indigenous cultures in the Mesoamerican area. Some of these other cultures are the Mexica (Aztecs), Mixtec, Purepecha, Huastec, Olmac, Toltec, Zapotec, and Teotihuacan.

These indigenous Mesoamerican cultures are credited with the creation and innovation of many inventions. They used advanced mathematics to engineer and build great pyramid temples that still stand after thousands of years. They were clear masters of observed astronomy and created highly accurate calendars. They maintained stable enough societies to allow the practicing of fine arts and integrated it into a complicated writing system that balanced both math and writing into a complex theology. The Maya are credited as being the first culture in the New World to utilize a fully developed written language.

They practiced elective medicine and for the most part, used an intensive agriculture system to maintain huge populations.

The Mesoamericans had discovered the wheel, but the absence of draft animals and an often demanding terrain made human labor the most utilized means for the transportation of goods and building materials. Suitable bovine or equine were not introduced into the Americas until later when Europeans brought them over.

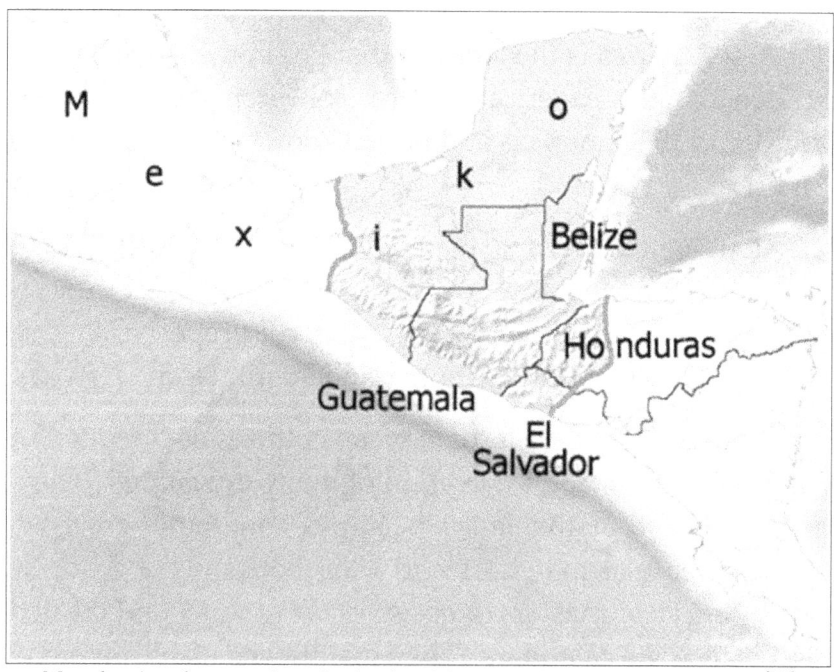

Map showing the area where the Ancient Maya were located in Mesoamerica.[235]

The areas dominated by the Maya are known today as the southern Mexican states: Chiapas, Campeche, Yucatan, Quintana Roo, and Tabasco. The Maya civilization spread all the way through the nations of Guatemala, Belize, El Salvador, and Honduras. A very large expanse of city-states that ruled the area linked by trade routes.

Descendants of the ancient Maya civilization live today in the Yucatán Peninsula of Southern Mexico, Guatemala, and parts of Honduras and El Salvador.

The proximity of the Mesoamerican people to each other in the region led to a high degree of cultural interaction between each other. The consistent interaction between Mesoamerican civilizations within the region created a cultural diffusion that allowed Mesoamericans to share a great degree of their cultural practices and knowledge with each other.

Mesoamericans continually influenced each other, even when their interaction wasn't always peaceful. The writing and epigraphy used to create the famous 'Maya Calender' weren't even of Maya origination. They had assimilated it into their own culture from neighboring cultures in their region.

The writing used in the region had come from previous cultures and evolved over time within each different Mesoamerican culture. Script and usage becoming slightly altered or modified as each unique scribe used it in relation to their own culture.

The Maya people were not necessarily known as being

great inventors themselves, but were instead great innovators that absorbed others advancements and continued to develop upon them within their own culture. The culture of the ancient Maya seemed to promote the application of inventions of the many other nearby cultures in the area and sought ways to improve upon them on their own.

Like many of the other Mesoamerican cultures, the Maya did not have a separation between religion and government. Church and State were one of the same. They considered the gods to be the everyday rulers of their daily lives and depended on their priests and rulers to ensure that the gods were appeased and didn't destroy the earth or extinguish the essential life sustaining Sun.

The Maya religion required a highly complicated method of worship that demanded bloodletting and sacrificial rituals that were often fulfilled by the kings and queens. These efforts were necessary because it was believed to "feed" the gods. It was the sacred duty and responsibility of the ruler to often feed the gods with their own blood. The believed their rulers had the power to pass in and out body to the spirit world and acted as messengers to the celestial world.[109]

Geographically, the Maya were formed individually as independent city-states. They used a government structure that allowed their individual rulers a great deal of individual governance within their own municipalities, instead of a strong centralized governing structure ruled by an emperor or empress.

The Maya civilization wasn't a single unified empire, but were instead a multitude of separate entities that shared a common cultural background. They shared several similarities with the Greeks, in that the Maya were religiously and culturally a nation, but were politically separate sovereign city-states.

The city center of Tikal, one of the most powerful Classic Period Maya cities.[200]

Maya city centers were the epicenters for trade, religious, and other cultural activities which also included some local administration.[201] There were many Maya cultural centers located in what's considered "the Maya Area" that spreads across a large expanse covering a wide range of climate conditions. Their culture spanned across mountain ranges into semi-arid plains and reached into the thick labyrinths of the rain forests. A diverse area that allowed for a diversity of trade.

Map of the Maya Area in the Yucatán peninsula.[1]

The period of time before the arrival of Christopher Columbus and European expansion to the Americas is called the 'Pre-Columbian Period.' The Pre-Columbian period of Maya history divides into five distinct time periods.

- the Paleo-Indian Period ("First People" - 3500 BC),
- the Archaic Period (3500 BC - 2000 BC),
- the Preclassic Period (2000 BC - 200 AD),
- the Classic Period (200 AD - 900 AD),
- the Post Classic Period (900 AD - 1697 AD).

It was during the Paleo-Indian period when early nomads crossed into the Americas over 15,000 years ago. These were the "First People" to inhabit the Americas. They'd first crossed into North America until eventually splitting off from other groups and eventually migrating south through Mexico into the Yucatán Peninsula of Mesoamerica.

These migrating "First People" in the Maya region developed their tool and hunting technologies and went from being nomadic hunter-gatherers into forming more permanent settlements. These settled groups became more developed as they exploited the plentiful local resources.

These now settled groups progressed into the Archaic period and began advancing into a more complex society. These archaic settlements developed culture and technology that was shared with neighboring settled groups. The exchange of ideas between these groups formed into a shared culture that began developing into a culturally distinct people.

The Maya Civilization originated in the Yucatán region during the Preclassic Period at around 2000 BC. There is some argument as to when the Preclassic Period began for the Maya. It's argued to have began as late as 2600 BC, while there's claim that it's earlier because there are permanent Maya settlements along the Pacific coast that date to 1800 BC. A difference of eight hundred years, depending on region.

The Preclassic period begins where the first signs that the Maya can be recognized as a distinct people. The two time periods overlap each other as a result from different groups in the region gradually shifting from being a separate archaically developed people into adopting local culture and technology that was distinctly Maya.

It was also during the Preclassic period that the Maya developed a greater interest in art and began some degree of manufacturing. A number of Preclassic Maya pottery and clay figures that were fired in primitive kilns survive to this day. Many of these clay and pottery artifacts, that are well over four thousand years old, give us clues as to their origin and purpose. Indicators as to how advanced their technology was growing. The process of using buildings as a means of recording history had also began to develop during the Maya Preclassic era.

A very distinct Maya culture with religious beliefs and practices, as well as shared technologies, began to rapidly form and progress during the Preclassic period. Public ceremonies and rites begin taking place during the Preclassic period. The creation of burial rites for the dead began during this time. The Maya civilization continued to grow and advance into its Classical Period, where it reached its peak in development at around 200 - 250 AD. Still almost two thousand years before contact with Europeans.

The Classic Period for the Maya culture occurred from 200 to 900 AD. During this time, the Maya began to develop urban centers that were more focused on the pursuit of artistic and intellectual development. These city centers became true cultural hubs in various Maya city-states. Written documents from the Classical period demonstrate a highly developed method of communication amongst the Mesoamerican people. It was during the Classical period that engineering feats, such as the construction of pyramids in the city-states began emerging.

The desire to preserve personal and cultural histories begins to develop during the Classical period as well. There are many carved slabs of stone known as 'stelae' that have survived to tell the stories and lineage of important rulers of the time.

The Maya had developed a complex system of carved hieroglyphs to preserve the stories of historical events.

Maya Stelae and Pyramid located at the Copan Ruins in Honduras.[202]

Lidded effigy container in the form of a god, 1500 AD Late-Postclassic period.[213]

Towards the end of the Classic Period was when the structure of Maya society began to change. Settlements in the southern lowlands started dwindling in population until eventually becoming abandoned. This may be perhaps to natural disasters such as hurricanes known to the region. The architecture began appearing seemingly ordinary rather than having the elaborately ornate inscriptions that were apart of the buildings built centuries prior. Building took on a more utilitarian emphasis rather than the previous . There were few, if any, grand structures appearing in the 8th or 9th centuries leading into the Maya Post-classic Period.

During the Post-classic Period, the Maya people and their culture continued to thriving in the Northern sections of the Yucatan' area. Buildings in new settlements were now being constructed with plain straight walls and flat ceilings. These simple lines now characterized the construction of new buildings, in contrast to the elaborate carvings and decorations used in construction during the previous period.

The earlier interest in art continued to be part of Maya culture as well as a continued interest in language and writing, Yet the great bursts of creativity that came out during the earlier periods appear to have ceased during the Post-classic period of the Maya civilization.

Assimilation with other neighboring cultures had weakened some of the distinctiveness of Maya culture as they interacted more heavily on neighboring cultures. Nevertheless there were still several city-states that retained a decidedly distinctive Maya culture well into the 16th century.

During the Post-classic period the Maya civilization continued as a major dominating force for 700 more years until around 900 AD when their culture became less dominate in the region.

The Maya city-states continued through the arrival of the Spaniards in 1511 AD and continued until after almost two centuries of efforts by Spanish Conquistadors, the last Maya city was conquered in 1697 AD.

Even after the Spanish Conquest and subsequent colonization, the Maya people and the spoken Mayan language did not die out with the end of their civilization. The legacy of the Maya civilization lives on today in several ways. Many members of the rural populations in Chiapas, Guatemala, Belize, and the Yucatan Peninsula are Maya by descent and utilize one of the Mayan dialects as their primary verbal language.

The Culture of the Maya people can be found influencing many cultures around Mexico and other parts of Central America. Artifacts that are undeniably of Maya origin have been found as far away as Central Mexico, which is more than 1000 kilometers away.

Chapter 2

The Paleo-Indian Period (First People - 3500 BC)

In the history of Mesoamerica, the Paleo-Indian period applies specifically to when the very first indications of human habitation within the Mesoamerican region began. This is an event that took place during the stone age (paleolithic) stage of human evolution when migrating hunter-gatherers began permanently settling in areas.

The prefix "paleo" comes from the Greek adjective 'palaios' to describe something "old" or "ancient." The terms Paleo-Indian (Old Indian) or Paleo-Americans (Old Americans) refers specifically to the small bands of nomadic people whom first populated into the Americas during the final glacial episodes of the late Pleistocene period.

The Late Pleistocene period was when the final glacial episode of ice sheets covered much of the northern hemisphere. This event happened about 125,000 years ago and lasted until about 12,000 years ago.[237] Much of the Late Pleistocene age was dominated by glaciation. The land was taken over by towering sheets of ice such as the Wisconsin glaciation in North America and corresponding glacial periods in Europe and Asia. The towering glacial ice was impassable and reshaped the entire countryside.

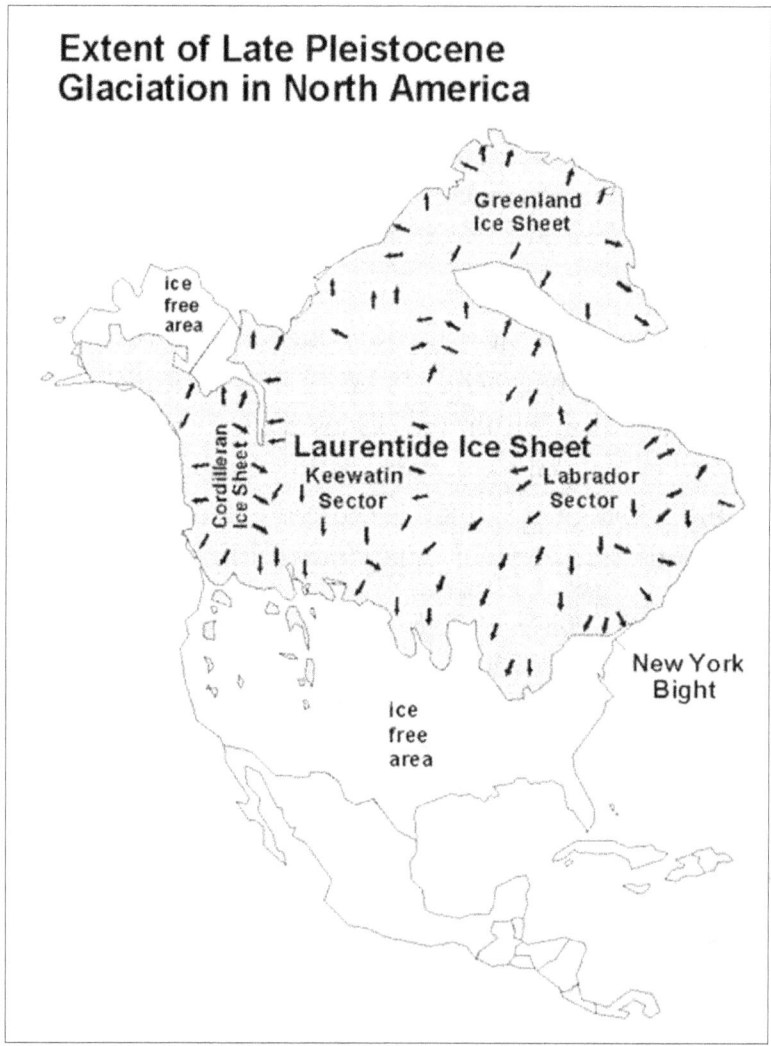

North American map showing Late Pleistocene glaciation.[236]

It wasn't until during the end of the Late Pleistocene period that the ice began to melt and the glaciers started to recede. It left land-ice bridges and these surviving human species were now able to cross and spread to every continent on Earth, except the Antarctica.

It was during the end of the Pleistocene period when the most recent episodes of global cooling from the last Ice Age took place. During this time much of the World's temperate zones were alternately covered by glaciers during cool periods and then uncovered during the warmer interglacial periods. During these warmer periods was when the glaciers retreated and allowed intercontinental passage.[110]

At the end of the last Ice Age, there were periods when sea levels lowered enough to create linking land and ice masses between Siberia and Alaska. These land-ice masses formed into what's called, "Beringia." The Beringia land-ice mass was about 580,000 square miles in range, which is roughly about twice the size of the state of Texas.

Beringia only existed when global sea levels fell enough to expose land masses that were joined together by ice. Beringia had existed during several periods in the Pleistocene time period.

During this time Beringia was connected to Siberia by a "bridge" made of land and ice. The Bering land-Ice bridge is believed to have existed both during the period glaciation that occurred more than 35,000 years ago and then again during a more recent period which lasted from 22,000 to

7,000 years ago. It was during the period between 16,000 to 12,500 years ago when the majority of humans crossed into the Americas from Siberia.[19]

Glacier Blocked Bering Land Bridge.[206]

The Bering land bridge allowed passage between the two continents until sea levels began rising when the climate once again changed. Radiocarbon dating tests reveal that sea levels had lowered more than 400 feet below today's current levels from the growth of immense ice sheets in the Northern Hemisphere during the Ice Age.

The last warming, about 6000 years ago, is when the coastlines assumed their approximate sea levels and configurations that exist today.[215]

When the fifty-five mile long Beringia land-ice bridge was exposed, it was for a period the usually lasted approximately 3500 years.[205] Three to four millennia is more than a sufficient amount of time to allow wandering humans and other wildlife, such as mammoths, to cross into the Americas.

Based on plant life found from sea-core samples taken, it is believed that the area was covered with tundra plants and shrubs rather than being an arid grassland. This means that Beringia no longer provided adequate grazing for large herds of grazing animals.[205]

Some fauna and megafauna that crossed over were able to adapt and survive on what grazing and flora was available. But not all, many animals simply died off as a result of the lack adequate food sources. Many species were simply were hunted out of existence.

Artist's depiction of Columbian Mammoths that roamed North America. [238]

The big game hunters followed animals such as bison, mammoth, and mastodon through the Bering Strait from Siberia into North America when the Beringia land-ice bridge was exposed.[19][36]

These migrating hunters from Asia and Siberia became the Paleo-Indians to first occupy Beringia leading the way into North America.

Paleo-Indians butchering a bison at the end of the Ice Age.[214]

After they crossed over, rising sea levels and ice blocked their way back to Siberia. The land-ice bridge that allowed them to cross over was now gone. They couldn't return and glacial ice also blocked their passage further into the Americas. The first human entrants into the Americas had become trapped on Beringia for about 20,000 years.

Several generations had remained in Beringia until the ice receded to allow passage into the Americas.[208] During this period of time many megafauna had become extinct. Species of humans other than modern humans had either died out or were bred out during the Pleistocene glacial period.

The genetic traits that distinguish all Native Americans from non-native Americans had evolved during this twenty thousand year stay in Beringia. This period of isolation from other humans made a unique Native Americans. They are still similar to East Central Asians genetically, but have noticeable differences. Twenty thousand years is more than sufficient time to create the genetic polymorphisms that are distinguishably Native American.[208][209]210]

In many ways, indigenous Americans are linked to Asianics, specifically to eastern Siberian populations. The distribution of blood types and DNA link indigenous Americans to Asianics.[22] They are also linked by linguistic elements.

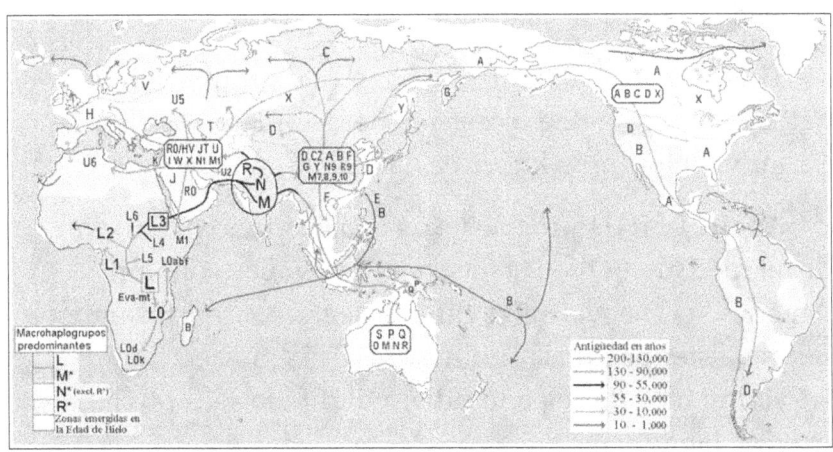

Hypothesized map of human migration based on mitochondrial DNA.[203]

After a long period of time the glaciers began to melt. The glaciers diminished rapidly enough that it could be seen over a person's lifetime. When the glaciers began melting and receding, the path into the New World opened. Beringia was no longer blocked by ice. However, the way back to Siberia was blocked by the sea. So the surviving humans and animals on Beringia migrated into the Americas.

Some of the earliest human settlements in North America were thousands of years before the latest glacial period when the land-ice bridge existed.[38] There were humans living in the northern parts of the Yukon area of Beringia when it was glacier-free 32,000 years ago.[39][40]

There were small groups of people that had passed through the Bering land-ice bridge as early as 40,000 years ago. Some of the first migrants to make it into the Americas. Most of the migration into the Americas occurred 15,000 years ago. This was when migration through Beringia was simpler when the glacial ice had literally broken and opened large access paths into the Americas.

These new inhabitants were isolated groups of hunter-gathers that migrated alongside herds of large herbivores far into what is now known as Alaska.

About 18,500 to 15,500 years ago, ice-free corridors also developed along the Pacific coast and valleys of North America.[20] The warming climate began to transform the Beringia steppe into shrub tundra. This pushed the surviving megafauna and other wildlife to seek out better grazing lands.

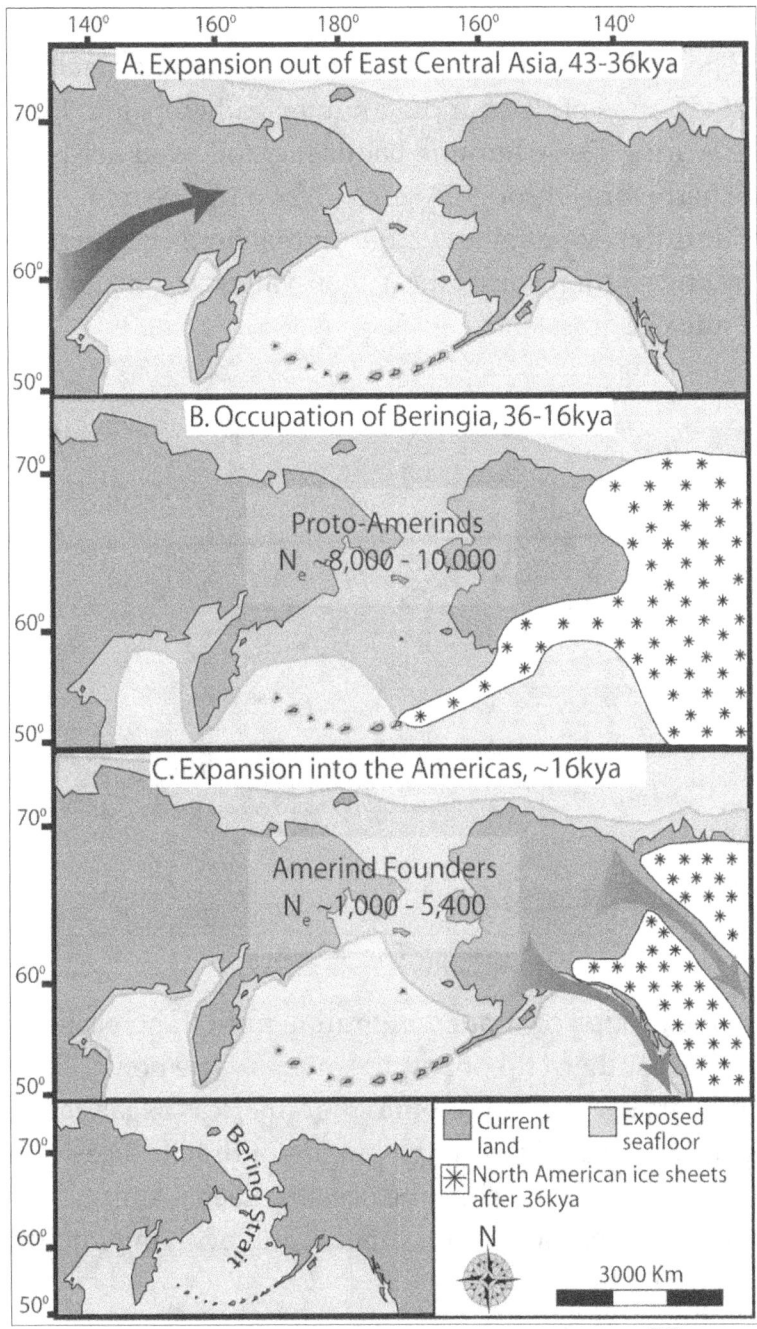

The phases of initial American migration by Paleo-Indians.[211]

The dwindling food sources also pushed the small isolated bands of Paleo-Indian hunter-gatherers into the New World. These hunting bands had followed herds of large herbivores through Alaska. When the ice free corridors developed, these large animal herds began migrating south through the Yukon Valley and made their way into the grasslands.

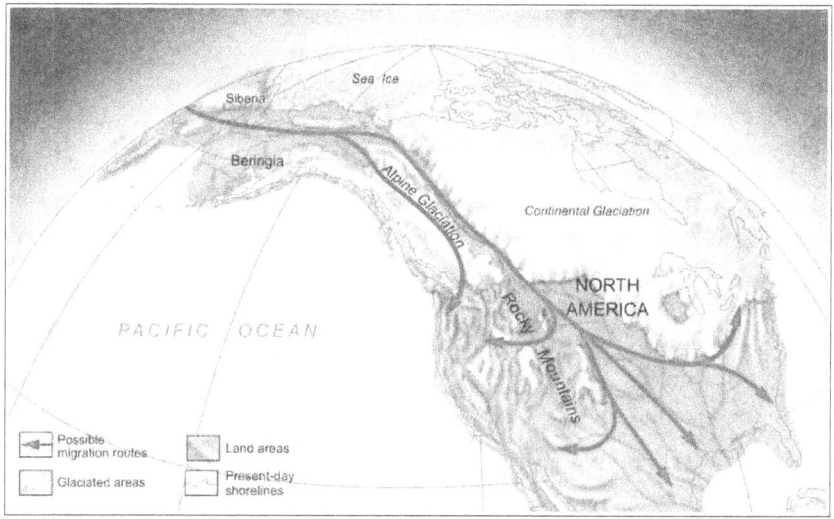

Migration of Paleo-Indians.[206]

Some groups continued migrating until they reached as far as the southern tip of South America. The new inhabitants had spread out into the Americas as far east as Virginia and past through the jungles of Brazil. They only stopped when the reached the oceans. Each group adapting to their new environments and evolving into their own distinct cultures.

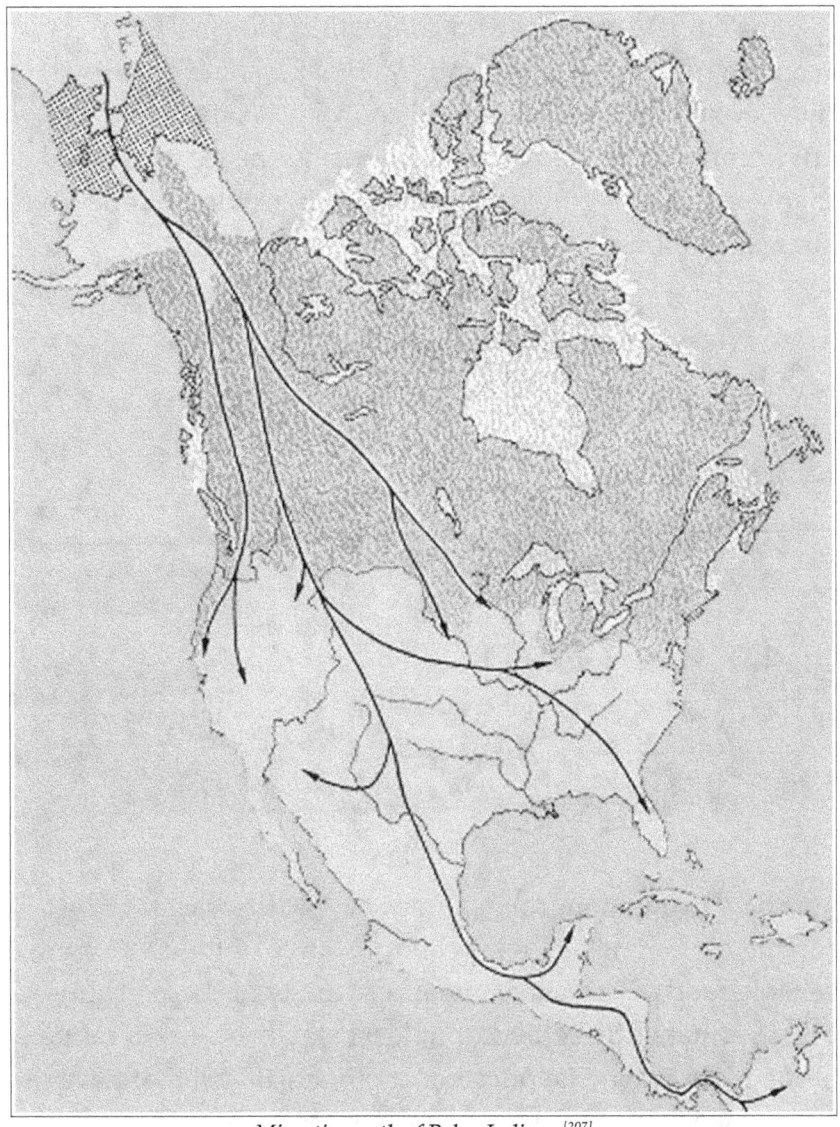
Migration path of Paleo-Indians.[207]

People from this period of time generally concentrated on hunting various large game as their primary food source, but they also foraged for locally available foods.

The climate changes and competition for food sources would have caused longer migrations for some groups as they looked for consistent food sources. As the environment changed around them and the ice age ended, many animals migrated great distances seeking out new sources of food.[35]

Paleo-Indians hunting a glytodont.[23]

Some groups migrated along the Pacific coastal areas relying on fishing as their primary source of food.[37] With reliable food sources in some areas, many of these groups even permanently settled or at least stay in a certain range. Stone tools, projectile points and other artifacts that have been discovered give us evidence of the earliest human activity.

The types of artifacts, such as projectile points used with arrows and spears, tell us the approximate date and level of technology developed by early humans.

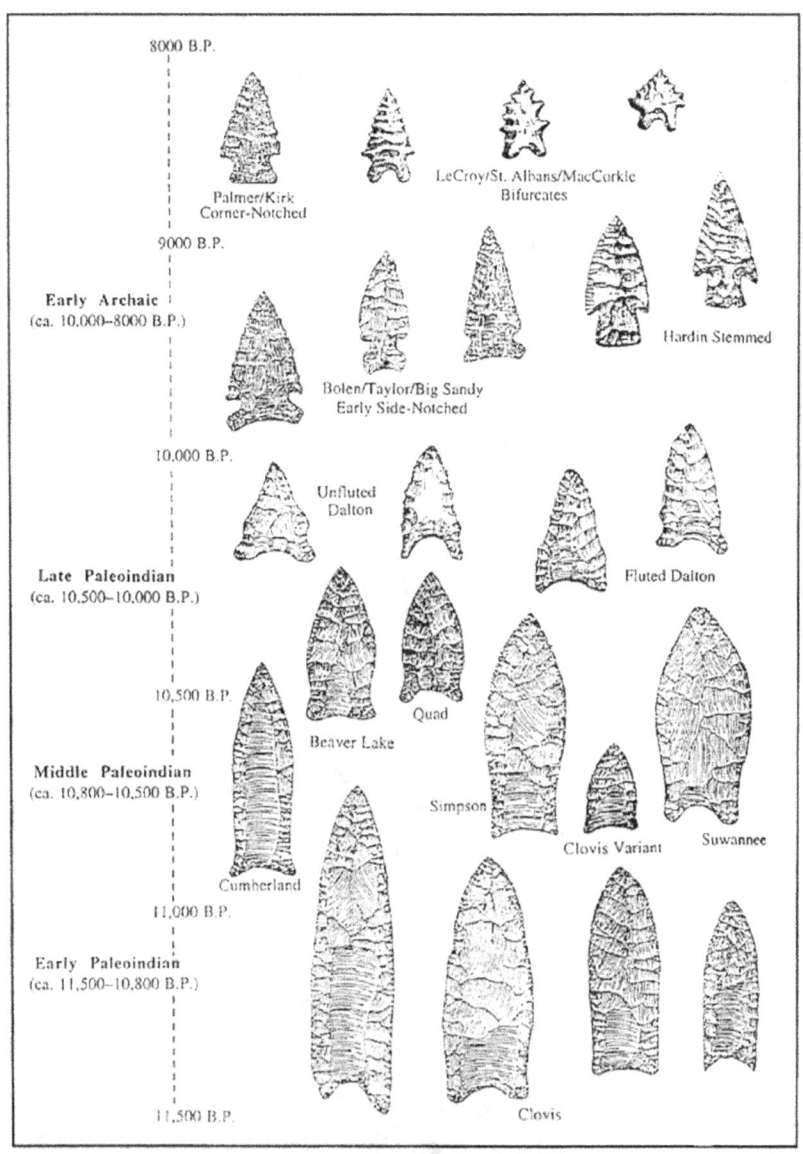

Paleo-Indian Projectile Point Types.[204]

Crafted stone age flaked tools (projectile points being the most commonly discovered) are used by researchers to classify the development of cultures and periods of use.[21]

Around 10,000 to 9000 years ago the climate stabilized and this led to a rise in population. Advances in Stone Age technology resulted in a more sedentary lifestyle. Humans began to settle in small groups populated by game and other stabilize food sources. The permanent peopling of the Americas had occurred by 9,200 BC.[24][25]

This time period in Mesoamerican history is referred to as the "Paleo-Indian period." This is the period when early human migration into the Mesoamerican region took place. A period of time that ranged roughly from 12,000 to 7000 years ago.

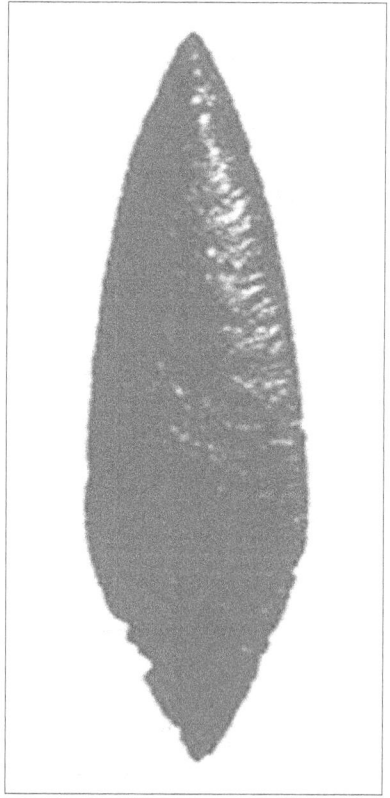

Paleo-Indian obsidian projectile point from 9500 BC found in Guatemala.[26]

Paleo-Indians are generally classified by their level of progression in stone age technology. The level of advancement in lithic or stone age technology used by these people is evaluated by the variety of techniques they used to produce various tools from stone. How advanced in the manufacturing and sophistication of tool making and types of tools they used.

Stone tools such as spear points and other projectile points would typically be made by chipping flakes from stone. Mesoamerican Paleo-Indians had the advantage of access to obsidian, which could be chipped into very sharp tools.

Atlatl weights and carved stone gorgets from Poverty Point.[31]

Fluted spear points were constructed from chipped stones with a long groove in the center added called a "flute." The fluted spear point was then tied on to the end of a spear or other projectile weapon. These weapon shafts were usually made from wood or bone.[32][33][34]

Man-made fluted points have been found in northern Mesoamerica in the Mexican states of Sonora and Durango. The remains of a mammoth hunt have been discovered near Mexico City at Santa Isabel Iztapan and at Los Reyes la Paz.

Cranial discoveries also show early human presence in Mesoamerica during this period of time. In many locations, skulls have been found belonging to early Mesoamerican Paleo-Indians with remains of fauna and stone age artifacts made of obsidian. Discoveries showing evidence of a Paleo-Indian hunters, their prey, and the weapons and tools they used.

The Paleo-Indian time period lasts through until the onset of permanent settlements, agricultural development and other proto-civilization traits that lead into the Archaic time period in Mesoamerican history.

Chapter 3

The Archaic Period (3500 BC - 2000 BC)

The archaic stage was the second stage of cultural development in the Americas. The archaic stage is when most cultures began living more settled lives in contrast to continual migrating in search of food. They began improving their tools and used baskets for food gathering and storage. The beginning stages of agriculture come at this stage.

The period of time it took one culture to progress into this stage of cultural evolution varied from one group to another. Each culture's needs and availability to stable resources varied from one location to another.

This stage of development took place for most cultures in the Americas anywhere from around 8000 BC to 2000 BC. Cultures that relied on fish and other stable local food sources were more likely to transition faster into this stage than others. Some groups continued to migrate and maintained a life of hunting and gathering to survive.

The Mesoamerican Archaic Period is characterized by subsistence economies that were supported through the regular exploitation of local food stuffs such as: nuts, seeds, and shellfish in addition to local hunting.

There are numerous different variations of these substance economies that have been identified. For example, the southwestern archaic cultures are subdivided into the Dieguito-Pinto, Oshara, Cochise and Chihuahua cultures.[217] They are subdivided because these cultures developed at different times and relied on slightly different regular food sources.

Dating a culture's progress is difficult at best and is highly dependent on rare finds. Archaic sites found in Northern Louisiana, Mississippi, and Florida show that many hunter-gatherer societies in the Lower Mississippi Valley region not only interacted with each other but traded and shared technologies. They had even organized together to build monumental mound complexes that date back as early as 3500 BC.

They continued to build these mound complexes for over half a millennium. Mound sites such as the ones found at Frenchman's Bend and Hedgepeth were of this time period and were all of localized societies.

The Watson Brake archaeological site in Ouachita Parish, Louisiana is considered to be the oldest mound complex in the entire Americas.[218] We can only speculate that these practices not only united some communities, but may have been the start of what would have eventually evolved into the Maya pyramid structures.

The Watson Blake site is nearly 2,000 years older than the site at Poverty Point, which is also located in Northern Louisiana. There are more than 100 regional sites associating with the Poverty Point culture of the Late Archaic period. These cultures regularly interacted with each other and had a regional trading network that connected to other cultures across the Southeast of North America.

Across the region of the Southeastern part of North America about 6,000 years ago, cultures were exploiting wetland resources and left behind large shell middens. These shell middens contained debris of human activity. Some of the shell middens discovered were processing areas where aquatic resources were processed directly after being harvested for use or stored in a distant location. Some shell middens were village dump sites. A treasure trove for archaeologists that get to collect information by items left behind or discarded by early archaic cultures.

Some middens found were directly associated with a house within a village. Each household would dump its garbage directly outside the house. These dump sites contain detailed records of what foods were processed and eaten. Often there would be fragments of stone tools and other household goods. Objects that are invaluable to archaeological studies.

Archaic period shell middens are numerous in the South Carolina and Georgia coastal regions. They're scattered around the Florida Peninsula and along the coast of the Gulf of Mexico. Resources were rich enough in these regions that it was able to support sizable mound-building communities all year-round.[219][220]

Archaic period sites across Mesoamerica resemble the same building methods and technology used by other groups spread throughout the Southwestern and Southeastern regions of North America.

Artist's depiction of an Archaic period village.[224]

Paleo and Archaic era groups carried influenced technologies from these groups with them as they migrated into the Mesoamerican region. These were the hunter-gather groups that were beginning to settle and merge into archaic settlements. These groups learned and developed near similar technological concepts and ideas within their own cultural practices. These cultural practices developed into being distinctively Mesoamerican.

The changed climate and an ever increasing human population with hunting techniques that continually improved, the large animals in the Americas began to perish. By 8,000 years ago, two-thirds of all North American animals weighing more than 100 pounds were now extinct. The Ancient Bison (bison antiquus) was the only large animal to survive on the vast ranges of the Great Plains.[221][222]

Artist's depiction of an Archaic Camp Scene.[223]

During the Archaic period a warmer and much more arid climate, in addition to excessive hunting, saw an end to the last megafauna in the Americas. Besides the bison, the great beasts that the first migrants for so long relied upon for sustenance were now gone.[27]

The majority of the population were in groups of highly mobile hunter-gatherers. But now some of these individual groups began to settle as they started to focus on resources available to them locally. As time passed these groups became permanently settled and shared knowledge, customs, and beliefs with neighboring groups.

These early settled groups progressed into the Basketmaker Era of the Archaic cultural period. This was when some groups became distinguishably different from other archaic settlements by the basketry they used to gather and store food.

These archaic basket weaving groups became reliant on wild seeds, grasses, nuts and fruit for food. Often they'd changed their movement patterns and lifestyle in order to maximize gathering the edible wild food and small game within a geographical region.

With the extinction of megafauna, hunters had adapted their tools and began using spears with smaller projectile points. They began using the atlatl and darts for smaller game. Shelters and other simple dwellings were made out of wood, brush and earth. The entirety of their lifestyle changed as they improved upon adapting to their settled environments.

Many archaic groups progressed into planting and using agricultural crops. Typically they grew maize, beans, and squash. Their agricultural methods gradually improved over time as their settlements grew larger and agriculture became a more reliable and important source of subsistence.[78]

There was still an absence in these archaic cultures of any formal social stratification. There isn't any form of writing or any major architecture structures being built beyond mound building.

Agriculture continued to develop as permanent villages established themselves in the region. Later in this period the use of pottery and loom weaving became common. Societal class divisions also began to appear in some settlements. The late archaic period is when basic technologies in terms of stone-grinding, drilling, and pottery were established in Mesoamerica.

Regional adaptations to common skills and technologies became the norm during the late archaic time period. Many groups continued as game hunters, but their hunting methods became more sophisticated. Other methods of procuring food became more complex as well.

Most groups became less reliant on traditional hunting and gathering practices. They now had growing mixed economies of small game, fish, seasonally gathered wild vegetables and other harvested foods. Harvesting food to trade with other settled groups for other food stuffs was now common.[28][29][30]

A culture's progression out of the archaic stage is defined by their adoption of sedentary farming. This progression varied significantly across the Americas; but by 2000 BC, the majority of Mesoamerican cultures had made their transition out of the archaic stage.[216]

Chapter 4

Preclassic Maya (2000 BC – 200 AD)

The Maya Preclassic period is divided into three time periods: the Early Preclassic, the Middle Preclassic, and the Late Preclassic period. The Preclassic Period of Maya history begins where the first settlements have evidence of crop cultivation. This period began from around 2000 BC to 2600 BC and lasted until around 200 AD to 250AD.

Most Maya groups had already transitioned out of the archaic period and were already becoming distinguishably Preclassic Maya. Their cultural practices which were now unique to their people and they had built agricultural based settlements.

The earliest Maya came into the tropical lowland areas around modern day Belize as farmers before the Preclassic period over 4,000 years ago. These ancient Maya started building their storied cities in MesoAmerica as early as 1000 BC.[276]

The Early Preclassic Period marks the beginnings of agriculture. These are the settled groups that slowly grew into settlements that improved upon their knowledge of growing foods. Their settlements grew in size because of reliable agricultural methods that were able to provide sustenance for their growing populations.

Some sample varieties of maize cultivated by the Maya.[245]

Knowledge of maize use and cultivation was passed on from one group to another throughout the Southwestern portion of North America. This agricultural knowledge was carried into Mesoamerica by migrating farmers whom brought their learned farming methods with them. The knowledge was gradually shared through interaction between other groups. [245]

There are differences in cultivation techniques used by different groups and even different words used for maize.

These differences in cultivation methods and terminology tell us that their methods developed after these groups had already settled into early organized societies. Their maize culture differed from that of other groups across the Americas.

The time it took some Mesoamerican groups to transition into an agricultural culture stretched over a period of nearly two thousand years. The abundance of local foods that was readily available made cultivation and general agriculture something that was adopted slowly. Most of their dietary proteins were obtained primarily from the meat of local game. There was no great need to adopt agriculture until growing populations demanded it.

The earliest regular planned cultivation of maize in the Maya area dates before the Preclassic period. In Guatemala, evidence of early field burning has been found that dates before 2000 BC. These field burnings were most likely done annually, which is a practice used to ready crop fields for the following Spring.

There is pottery and architecture that date from 2000 BC to 1000 BC associated with this phase of Preclassic culture. In Belize, this kind of field burning agriculture and other soil manipulation methods had been used by early preclassical Maya. Additionally ceramic items have been found in these site locations that also date to the Preclassic period.

The early preclassic era Maya agriculturalists in Belize had grown domesticated maize, fruits, cacao and a variety of root crops. Yet their diet was only partly supplied by these domesticated crops. There was still a high dependence on the readily available foods that could be acquired locally through hunting, fishing, and plant foraging. These food sources were an important part of the first Maya's diet. Social organization was predominately family-centered and based on subsistence.

The Middle Preclassic period was between 1000 BC and 300 BC. There are numerous Middle Preclassic settlement sites across most of the Maya area that easily date archaeologically to this period. During this time, the Maya ultimately spread into the interior areas when many moved up the river valleys from the coast. Hurricanes most probably being the main motivator for moving inland.

Communities were still small and sites discovered where they built houses were wide spread. The more significant communities in the Middle Preclassic period were in the interior regions which became the heartland of the Maya civilization. These were the communities that later became prominently developed with public architecture built during the Classic Period.

Public architecture began being built in these settlements when their populations grew significantly larger, such as the sites found in Cuello, Cerros, Nohmul, and Lamanai in northern Belize.

The Belize River Valley area had scattered houses with public platforms in their local centers. Middle Preclassic period buildings have also been found in Cahal Pech, Pacbitun and at El Pilar.

From 300 BC to 250 AD during the late preclassic period, the lowland Maya population continued to expand which resulted in greater competition for land and resources. This competition led to increased population densities in the larger Maya settlements and surrounding areas.

It became necessary to develop better resource and agricultural management strategies. The Maya began developing more complex and elaborate ways for coordinating, organizing, and feeding their growing populations.

This required the establishment of leadership in the form of Maya aristocracy with its corresponding societal hierarchy. This new ruling institution and its dynasties would shape the history of the Maya people through the Postclassic Period.

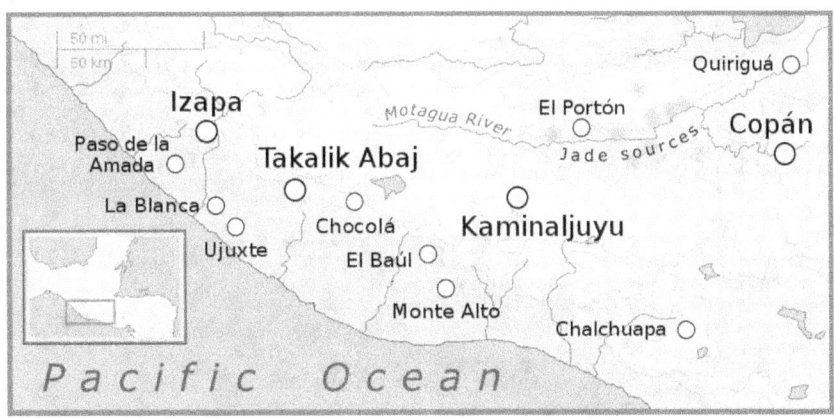

Preclassic sites in the lower Maya area.[246]

Many settlements gradually grew into major Maya city-states such as the ones in Izapa, Copan, Kaminaljuyu and El Mirador. Many of these city-states grew to being very prominent and powerful. Influencing their surrounding settlements and ruling families of different city-states often conducted warfare against each other.

The city-state of El Mirador grew to prominence and united with other states in the Maya lowlands. El Mirador dominated the lowlands until its decline and the city was eventually abandoned somewhere around 100 to 300 AD.

It's possible that the rulers of El Mirador became the Kaan Dynasty of Calakmul[2] Rivaling the city-state of Tikal in power and influence, Calakmul would become one of the two dominate powers of the Preclassical Maya era.

The Lost City of the Maya, El Mirador."[247]

Calakmul was one of the largest and most powerful of the ancient preclassic maya city-states. Calakmul is the city-state's modern name, in preclassic times it was known as "Ox Te' Tuun."

Calakmul was a major Maya power within the northern Yucatan region of southern Mexico. The dynasty of Calakmul administered over a large domain known as the Kingdom of the Snake. The snake head sign, which read as "Kaan." The emblem glyph of the Snake Kingdom was marked everywhere within their domain.[79]

A fragmented block at El Palmar represents an emblem glyph of Kaan, the Snake Dynasty of Calakmul.[80]

The Late Preclassic Period was one of major activity and cultural change. The population in the interior around the city-state of Tikal, modern day Guatemala, was dense since its rise to dominance. The Maya were also already engaged in early monument building projects at this time. There were considerable public constructions at major locations at Tikal and other interior centers. They used their newly merged surrounding communities to consolidate power and expand their influence.

The city-states of Nohmul, Lamanai, El Pilar and Cerros also grew to their peaks of power. They commanded the loyalty of large domains that contained many well established settlements and were firmly rooted by end of the preclassic period. Major public constructions of platforms and pyramids are found throughout different sites of these great preclassic era city-states.

Map of Preclassic Maya sites.[248]

Chapter 5

Early Preclassic (2000 BC - 1000 BC)

The Early Preclassic Era is the time period when the beginnings of agriculture emerge in Maya culture. The earliest evidence of agricultural field burning and cultivation of maize along with other crops dates well before the beginning of the Early Preclassic period. Agriculture was already being practiced in some areas of Guatemala that were settled by distinctively Maya groups.

The very roots of Maya civilization are obscure at best. However as our understanding of new and old discoveries increases, we're more able to paint a vague picture of their early beginnings. By around 2000 BC, the southern Maya area had already been occupied by early speakers of Mayan languages. We know that this area was occupied by archaic Maya groups prior to the early preclassic era. The first more permanent settlements were already beginning.

It was during the early preclassic period when the Maya culture transitioned from hunter-gatherers into agricultural based communities. They'd began experimenting with cultivating a variety of food bearing and edible plants. These grown crops were already become a major component of Maya diet. They grew a selection of root crops, domesticated maize and fruits. Cacao had not only made it into their diet but also was sometimes used as a form of currency.

But even with the presence of agriculture, grown crops still only made up for less than 30% of their diet. Fish, meat from hunting and other gathered foods still made up for the majority of their diet.[3] During the early preclassic period, the Maya at Cuello subsisted primarily on shell fish, deer and several small mammals in the local area. They supplemented their diet with corn, beans, squash and a variety of other plant foods. So even though these Maya settlements had transitioned into early preclassical agriculture, they retained a degree of their archaic hunter-gathering practices.

When agriculture gradually began to develop, so did the appearance of basic pottery. The Maya developed early pottery in simple design using a type of ceramics called "swasey." This type of pottery is relatively simple in form and predominantly reddish in color. These types of ceramic artifacts are what help us date these settlements specifically to the early preclassic era.

North of the progressing Maya, in the area of modern day Tabasco, Mexico, the Olmec culture was advancing. The presence of these Olmecs would have a profound impact on Maya society and culture. The early Maya began trading and interacting with the more advanced Olmec over a prolonged period. This contact altered the Maya way of life in almost every aspect.

The Olmecs were the first significant civilization to develop in Mesoamerica. They are essentially the mother culture of pre-Hispanic Mexico. The Olmec people were also known by other groups as the "rubber people."

Their religious beliefs venerated the jaguar as a supernatural being. There are Olmec artifacts which bear the images of the were-jaguar. The were-jaguar combined the physical characteristics of both humans and felines. These artifacts have been found scattered in several locations throughout Mexico. The were-jaguar artifacts show just how far the influential reach of Olmec culture was in Mesoamerica. Various Olmec-like symbols that were carved and painted on their relatively more sophisticated pottery have been found half way up the Mexican Gulf coast in the state of Veracruz.

In the lowlands near the Gulf Coast of the Mexican states of Veracruz and Tabasco are remains of Olmec ceremonial centers. An important Olmec political and religious center that flourished between 1200 and 900 BC is located in the Coatzacoalcos River basin of San Lorenzo.

The Olmec had also built the first conduit drainage system known in the Americas. An amazing advancement in engineering, but the Olmec are best known for the six colossal basalt heads. These massive stone heads are eight to nine feet in height and weigh from twenty to forty tons each.

These colossal heads were carved from stone that were

obtained more than 50 miles away and were brought to the site. A monolithic undertaking for a post stone age / early agricultural people. These stone monolith faces have noticeably negroid facial features, even though they are uniquely Olmec in origin.

Olmec Colossal Head 3 in San Lorenzo. [239]

The Colossal Heads also appear to be wearing helmets, something that has puzzled researchers ever since they were discovered. The first Olmec head was discovered at Tres Zapotes where at the same time 'Stelae C' was discovered. Markings on Stelae C bear the Olmec calendar long count date which converts to 31 BC. This date on the stelae gives us a probable date for the placement of the Colossal Head.

More gigantic heads like the one at Tres Zapotes, in

addition to a number of massive stone altars and stelae, have been discovered at the La Venta site. This site was the Olmec people's most important cultural center. It was their capital city, the cultural heart of their society. These massive stone works were somehow floated by means of using waterways to La Venta. The La Venta site is located on an island near the Gulf Coast in the present-day Mexican state of Tabasco.

The Olmec center at La Venta shares essential characteristics with all Mesoamerican centers later built by different cultures in the area. The site is laid out along a north and south axis with a huge earth and clay pyramid as its most prominent feature.

The Olmecs were a very advanced culture for their time. They were the first Mesoamerican people to understand the concept of zero, which is essential in mathematics. They were the first to develop a calendar and were the first to create an hieroglyphic writing system to record events. The Olmec's intellectual achievements, religious beliefs and rituals were very influential on the neighboring cultures around them. Cultures such as the Maya, Zapotec, Mixtec and Aztec were all heavily influenced by Olmec culture.

Many Mesoamerican communities appear to have been permanently occupied prior to 1200 BC. It is within this period of the early preclassic period that the earliest Maya villages were found to be occupied in northern Belize. The settlement in Cuello was also settled by Maya around 1200 BC. This was a time in when the heavily Olmec influenced Maya began to come together as a city builders.

Their early settlements were now being built with a greater sense of permanence. The early settlement inhabitants even erected their thatch houses on low apsidal shaped (oval) platforms. These platforms were constructed using a lime-gravel mixture called sascab, in addition to using white lime and stone.

Although most of the structures in their settlements were residential homes, but a few structures were built as shrines specifically where important rituals were conducted by members of the community. Religion in the form of Mesoamerican blood rituals was now firmly a part of Maya culture. One structure found at the Cuello site had contained more than 20 skeletal remains of individuals whom may have been sacrificed to commemorate the construction of the community's holy shrine.

The first Maya settlers in Cayo also appear to have also moved into the area at around 1200 BC as had other Maya. They established their settlements on the hills along the major river systems. They built communities on the hilltop where they farmed the rich alluvial valleys, also collecting jute and hunted wild game. Like the colonizers of Cuello, the early Maya in the Belize River Valley constructed large and small apsidal shaped platforms on which they built wattle and daub buildings with thatched roofs.

Maya buildings weren't without decoration, we've learned from fragments of preserved stucco at the Cahal Pech site that the plaster walls of these buildings were painted in red and white bands.

Their populations began to grow as their settlements

grew with them. Broad cultural changes and increases in urban activity in Mesoamerica because corn began providing enough calories to trigger a move to a more settled and urban existence.[278] The spread in population demanded denser city building as available real estate became more and more scarce. The ancient Maya started building their storied cities as early as 1000 BC.[278]

This was the beginning of what later became the well known tall Maya cities with their steep pyramids and ceremonial platforms.

1000 BC Ceremonial platform at Ceibal Guatemala.[279]

A ceremonial platform built at Ceibal, Guatemala that dates to around 1000 BC, appears to precede the pyramid and plazas built in the Olmec city of La Venta in Tabasco, Mexico, at around 800 BC. The Olmec center at La Venta appears to have been deliberately destroyed sometime around 400 to 300 BC. There has not been any discoveries of why, but speculation points to conquest by a neighboring culture that conquered and destroyed the Olmec along with their civilization.

Numerous other Maya sites and related ones on the Pacific Coast show signs of growing from settlements into cities with ceremonial centers at around 1000 BC. The date from 1200 to 1000 BC appears to be the period of time when most Maya settlements progressed into the early preclassic period and built either cities or large settlements. Their interaction with each other and other cultures helped to progress this.

The Early Preclassic Maya had regularly traded and exchanged goods with both local and distant people. They were able to import obsidian, jade and iron pyrite from different regions in Mesoamerica. They even acquired conch shells for jewelry and salted reef fish from the Caribbean coast. This trade and regular interaction between other cultures and other Maya settlements helped push their knowledge and technology ever further as they progressed into the middle preclassic period.

Chapter 6

Middle Preclassic (1000 BC - 400 BC)

The Maya middle preclassic period began around 1000 BC. During this same time in other parts of the World, David becomes king of the ancient Israelites and the Iron Age begins for much of Eurasia. Across the Pacific ocean, the ancient Japanese begin to cultivate rice. Everywhere in the World cultures were thriving.

This was the period of time when the roots of a complex Maya society began to steadily form and they became a more advanced people. A progression that occurred after centuries of agricultural village life and trade. Food abundance allowed for leisure time which allowed time for innovation and invention. Their settlements grew into cities and as their needs changed they built accordingly.

They were now building canals and irrigation systems that demanded planning and coordinated human effort. The organized use of manpower began to appear with increasing complexity and scale. Society changed and social classes formed.

Prestige items such as obsidian mirrors and jade mosaics began to appear, demanding a more extensive trade network that reached well past the boundaries of the Maya civilization. Social classes and privilege now existed within the kingdoms. The nobility made sure to firmly secure their position of privilege with the help of priests working to appease their gods and pacify the people.

A nobility structured religious culture had transformed the Maya into a ritualistic centered society. Central plazas and earthen mounds gradually began to be included in villages. Desperate to appease their gods, on occasion some of these religious structures would be enhanced by masonry.

A mound in La Blanca, Guatemala is more than 75 feet tall and contains a fragment of masonry that strongly resembles an Olmec style carving of a head. The neighboring Olmec culture had a profoundly strong influence on Maya Culture. Maya began to carve stone stelae during this period of the preclassic era. They adorned the stelae with portraits of rulers, but the carvings were still devoid of any kind of writing yet.

The stelae in the city-state of Copan in western Honduras mark royal dynasties of the kingdom. The site was known for its development in agriculture long before stone architecture began being built there in the 9th century BC. The Copan river valley was rich and fertile and the Maya of that region thrived. The bounty from the land was plentiful and able to support artisans to produce sculptures and other carvings.

Maya Stela, at Copan, Honduras[13]

Early sculptors used a variety of media, including stone, wood, stucco and clay. Unfortunately, many of these works of that were created with perishable materials have deteriorated and are rarely found by archaeologists.[4][5] There is an abundance of cultural information about the middle preclassic Maya that will forever be lost in time.

In the southeastern region of the Maya area at around 900 BC, the La Blanc city-state dominated the Pacific coastal region to around 600 BC when the kingdom's rule collapsed. This 300 year reign of the La Blanc Maya is called the Conchas phase. The Conchas phase's progression is measured by their changes in pottery.

Changes in ceramics give us an idea of their level of technological progress, such as the introduction of fine paste ceramics. There were few imported ceramics in the region. Those that were imported were few and less decorative. Most of the ceramics were produced locally.

Middle preclassic Maya pottery.

Religion appears to have been a dominate factor in preclassical Mesoamerican life, not just for the Maya but for all the surrounding cultures as well. One of the first temples in Mesoamerica had been built at around 900 BC. This temple was 150 x 90 meters at its base and stood over

25 meters tall.[6] A colossal structure that took planned engineering and coordinated man power to be built solely on the basis of religion.

Besides building massive structures such as temples, there has been various other types of religious paraphernalia found in household dig sites. Figurines are the most numerous items of religious paraphernalia found at many of the Preclassic Mesoamerican sites.

Ceramic seated male figurine and a ceramic female figurine, both of 600-900 AD.[14]

Many archaeologists and other researchers interpret the discovered figurines as being religious artifacts that were used in domestic rituals, Figurines such as these are especially used for ancestral veneration. ancestral veneration was a practice most probably carried over from Siberia from early Paleo-Indians, as it was commonly practiced throughout the Americas is a variety of forms. Besides appeasing household gods and venerating ancestors, figurines were also used to mark important milestones in the life-history of individuals. Especially that of important figures and rulers.[7][8][9][10][11]

Agriculture, architecture, and religion weren't the only things that dominated Maya life, warfare appears to have intensified during the middle preclassic period. Maya weaponry starts becoming more advanced. Maya rulers begin to be portrayed as warriors and heroes. Additionally, the appearance of mass graves and decapitated skeletons found belonging to this period are undeniable of evidence of battles.

The Maya did not maintain large standing armies as did the Greeks, Egyptians, or the Romans. Instead, they conscripted able-bodied men and boys to muster together a militia. These mustered militias would then be armed from centralized arsenals kept in public buildings. Usually they were armed with stone clubs, spears and fire hardened wooden axes with flint or obsidian blades on the edges.

Besides melee weapons, they were also armed with blowguns, javelins and other projectile weapons such as slings, bows and arrows, and Atlatl spear throwers. Maya soldiers typically carried long, flexible shields of hide or smaller rigid round shields, but this wasn't always the case for mustered militia as it was for private soldiers and personal guards of nobility and the elite.

Maya warrior from set of History Channel's "Warriors: Maya Armageddon."[84]

Many warriors wore body armor that was made from cotton vests that were stuffed with rock salt. This armor was so effective that hundreds of years later, Spanish conquistadors would shed their own metal armor in the sweltering rain forest in favor of these Maya salt rock filled cotton 'flak jackets.'

The Maya also had a war helmet made of pyrite stone called a "Kohaw." These unique helmets were only wore by special soldiers such as the Ajaws (or Ahau meaning 'Lord,' usually a nobility title) and Kaloontes (meaning supreme warrior or military ruler). An example of these 'Kohaw' helmets were found inside a queen's tomb in the El Perú site, also known as the 'Wak,' in northern Guatemala.

El Perú 14.8 cm clay figure with removable Kohaw helmet.[94]

The queen's tomb was uncovered at a site in the ancient Maya city-state of El Perú, which was the capital of the Wak Kingdom. It is believed that the queen's tomb belonged to none other than Lady K'abel whom was a military ruler of the Wak, or 'Centipede Kingdom,' between the years 672 to 692 AD.

The tomb was found in the ruins of the ancient city's main pyramid temple. Maya hieroglyphs in the tomb include the names: "Lady Water Lily Hand" and "Lady

Snake Lord." Both of these names are thought to refer to Lady K'abel, whom had governed the Wak kingdom for her family, the Kan. The Kan dynasty is better known as the Snake dynasty. The Snake dynasty was based in the Maya capital of Calakmul, located in what's now Mexico.

Even though Lady K'abel ruled with her husband, K'inich Bahlam, she held the prestigious title of Kaloonte, meaning 'supreme warrior.' This title gave her a higher authority than even her husband, the king.

Like many Noble families worldwide, the Snake dynasty had a policy of marrying off its princesses and noblewomen to the kings of vassal states like that of the Wak Kingdom to the Kan Dynasty. These royal unions were not only to consolidate power, but were also in favor of achieving a greater unity in the southern Maya Areas. To control the southern Maya region was also controlling the rich breadbasket area that also contained the coveted cacao bean.[76]

The cacao bean has been an extraordinary and intensively cultivated commodity of enormous importance in Mesoamerica. The Maya used cacao in their cuisine, religion and even used it as currency. It was a commodity of high value and importance to Mesoamericans everywhere.

Cacao was so coveted that there are actually carved stone sculptures and figurines from the southern Maya area in Guatemala that depict decapitation and other sacrifices performed that were associated with cacao. These stone sculptures representative the fierce warfare that was waged over this commodity. Hundreds of years later, Spanish Conquistadors would make reference to Mesoamerican natives always fighting over the production and distribution of the cocoa bean and its various processed forms.[77]

The Maya called cacao, "kakaw" and like most Mesoamericans, believed that it was the food of the gods. They boiled the cacao bean and then mixed it with various peppers and spices to make a drink out of it.

Christian nuns on missionary in Mesoamerica believed that the diabolical powers of chocolate were due to the chili peppers and spices, so they replaced them with vanilla, sugar and cream with delightful results. So delightful, that the nuns would spend all day making chocolate and not tend to their missionary duties and had to be forbade from making it.

Chapter 7

Late Preclassic (400 BC - 200 AD)

During the Late Preclassic period, populations throughout the Maya area continued to increase. Many new settlements were founded and they quickly grew in size. Settlements that had been established during the Middle Preclassic period, continued developing and grew even larger.

The Late Preclassic period saw the rise of two powerful states that rivaled each other in scale and monumental architecture later in the Classic period. These were the Maya city-states of Kaminaljuyu in the highlands and El Mirador in the lowlands.

There were many important city centers that laid along trade routes that interconnected the Maya. Trade reached from the highlands all the way to the coastal regions of Mesoamerica. This increased trade fostered contact with other communities and brought in new ideas that were constantly being exchanged from region to region.

It was during the Late Preclassic period that all the major achievements of ancient Maya civilization were in place. An extensive trade network allowed the regular exchange of ideas and the people of preclassic period were already developing as a complex culture.

Regular Maya Trade Routes.[249]

The late Preclassic Maya culture included the use of mathematics that were incorporated in the recording of time over long periods which allowed the creation and usage of calendars. Their own writing system progressed and spread with their culture.

It is during this time that the production of vertically standing monolithic rocks called stelae (singular stela) and other carved monuments such as alters were now being created. These monuments were initially produced in the highlands and along the Pacific coastal regions, but quickly spread to other regions. Stelae have been found throughout the Maya area in every major preclassic Maya settlement.

Various other permanent carving were also starting to be produced in other parts of the Maya region. A stucco mask tradition had formed in the lowlands of Belize and Peten with masks flanking the stairways of their temples.

During the Late Preclassic period elaborately carved monumental architecture becomes more common. The earliest corbelled vaults (false arches) were being carved within enclosed tombs by important temples.

Ceramic styles also become more uniform cross-regionally and the production of pottery that was painted in three or more colors becomes both widespread and popular. Most of the new painted pottery was placed in the tombs and burials of elite rulers whom were now displaying marked differences in status with their subjects.

Their stories and the significant events in their lives were now being depicted and dated by their calendars.

There have been surviving late preclassic murals that have provided important information regarding Maya religion and of the rituals they practiced for royal inaugurations that date to around 100 BC.

Mural from Maya House at Xultun, northern Guatemala.[83]

All of these carved altars, works of stelae, wall carvings and preserved stucco works have shown us how much the Maya's culture and technology has progressed. The Maya civilization was reaching its zenith of development in the late Preclassic period when a great portion of their civilization suddenly disappeared or perished.

It is well known that the Maya civilization had long disappeared and their culture long had been lost for over 500 years. This was the aftermath of the Spanish conquest of Mesoamerica by Spanish Conquistadors. But the Spanish reported that there were already Maya cites that had been abandoned long before they had even arrived. The Spaniards had found the ruins of cities that were completely abandoned with no trace of being recently inhabited.

The story of the mysterious lost civilization that seemed to suddenly collapse for unknown reasons has puzzled archaeologists for well over half a millennium. There were actually two 'collapses' of the Maya civilization. The first one was at the end of the Preclassic period and the well known second occurrence at the end of the Classic period with the arrival of the Spanish.

The first collapse was at the end of the late preclassic period with the systematic decline and abandoning of some major city-states such as the ones at Kaminaljuyu and El Mirador sometime around 100 AD.[12] It is unknown why these cities were abandoned and left in ruins. There are a number of theories as to why these cities may have become emptied, but there is little consensus. Some believe that it was possibly war between rival Maya city-states or even perhaps from neighboring civilizations. There could have been a pandemic of disease brought on by famine with over demanding populations that were not able to cope. There is also a probability that a natural disaster, such hurricanes, could have wiped these cities into ruin.

Although a portion of the Maya civilization had collapsed with an unexplained disappearance; the remaining Maya city-states continued to progress into the height of their culture during the Classic period.

Chapter 8

The Classic Period (200 AD - 900 AD)

During the Classic period, the ancient Maya culture was flourishing in Mesoamerica. They were at the height of their splendor. So of their architecture changed and they began constructing buildings that paid homage to their rulers and gave reverence to their ancestors. This was the Classic Maya Period, a time between 200 AD and 900 AD when city-states were expressing their power by creating unique architectural centers that in many ways were meant to replicate their cosmology.

Paying homage to important ancestors was critical to their beliefs. One of the most important social acts for a new king was to establish their relationship with the founder of their lineage. Rulers did so by sponsoring the creations of magnificent works of art that shown their link to the ancestors and gods.[81] These are some of the works that have left clues behind for us to explore and learn the about the Maya's story.

During most of the Classic period, the population of the

Maya people continued to grow, especially in and around urban centers of kingdoms and city-states. The Snake Kingdom of Calakmul had at least a population of 50,000 or more people under their governance during the Classic period.

The Snake Kingdom was a ruled by a powerful dynasty and reached as far as in places that were 150 kilometers away from its capital in Calakmul. The Snake Kingdom had built many structures. There are 6,750 ancient structures identified at Calakmul alone. The largest structure built by this dynasty was the great pyramid at the Calakmul site. The Great Pyramid of Calakmul is also known as 'Structure 2.' It is one of the tallest of all the Maya temple pyramids.

The Great Pyramid at Calakmul.[82]

Most historians mark 300 AD as the beginning of the Maya Classic period because this was when the appearance of stelae began. The earliest stela dates to 292 AD. A stela is a carved vertical stone statue of an important king or ruler.

Stela of the Great King Waxaklajun Ubaah K'awii (18 Rabbits)in Copan.[225]

Stelae include not only a likeness of the ruler, but they also have a written record of his accomplishments in the form of glyphs carved on stone. Stelae became common in the larger Maya cites that thrived during this time. The Maya began to build multistoried temples, pyramids and palaces during this period of time. Many of the temples they had built were aligned with the Sun and stars. With the aid of their accurate calendars they would plan important ceremonies that took place when the temples were aligned with the right celestial objects.

This was a time in Mesoamerica when many forms of art thrived. Maya artisans were creating finely carved pieces of jade. They painted large murals and created finely detailed stone carvings in many forms. They also made finely painted ceramics and pottery that have survived to this day and time. Their level of complexity and artistic creativity was at an all time high.

During the year 258 AD, the Tutul-Xius, a princely family from Tulha, suddenly left Guatemala and appeared in the Yucatán Peninsula. It is uncertain as to why they had migrated and if it was related to the portion of the Maya civilization that had mysteriously collapsed in that part of the region. They may have been seeking refuge from war, the reason is never told in any of the recordings found of the Tutul-Xius family.

The Tutul-Xius had won over the good will of the Mayapan king and pledged themselves as his loyal vassals. The Tutul-Xius family, then founded the cities of Mani and Tihoo, They also founded the great city of Mérida which came with all its splendor. This architecture of this city displays the height and beauty of the Classical period Maya civilization.

Like many Greek city-states, the Maya city-states had their own gods they revered as favoring the inhabitants of the city. Keeping these gods happy, kept the whole Maya World happy.

In the city of Tihoo, 'Baklum-Chaam' was the deity most revered. Backlum Chaam was the god of male sexuality. He was the Maya version of the Greek god Priapu. The Maya had built a great temple as a sanctuary to this god.

Many of the larger cities and capitals had multiple gods to appease, including the greater gods. In the city of Izamal, a great pyramid was built to the Maya Sun God named, "Kinich-Kak-Mo." The Maya called this sacred temple, "Yahan-Kuna," meaning 'most beautiful temple.'

The city of Mérida was considered one of the most advanced Maya cites that contained some of the most beautiful buildings in the whole extent of country. This was how by the Spanish described it when they came upon this city a thousand years later. They were in awe of its beauty and the splendor of the city's elaborate architecture.

The Spaniards described some of the buildings as being thirty feet high and made of finely constructed hammered stone that was laid without cement. On the summits of these elaborately decorated buildings were four apartments. Each apartment was divided into 20 x 10 foot cells that had vaulted ceilings.

The Spanish priests were so pleased with the beauty of this architecture that they established the convent of St. Francis in Mérida and transformed the Maya temple into a Christian chapel for the service of God.[89]

This was how the Maya were building their cities by the Classic period. They were built in such a way that the Spanish were impressed with them over a thousand years after they were built.

Mérida wasn't the only Classic period Maya city rising to greater splendor. Arriving from the west, a prince named Cukulcan established himself at Chichen-Itza and took control of the supreme government of the Snake empire. He established Mayapan as the empire's capital city.

The Great Pyramid in the Maya city of Chichen Itza.[108]

By Cukulcan's management, the government was divided into three absolute sovereignties. These sovereignties would upon occasion act together and form one. The seven succeeding sovereigns of Mayapan embellished upon this king's ideas and improved the country, making Mayapan very prosperous.

At this time the city of Uxmal, governed by one of the Tutul-Xius, began to rival the city of Mayapan in extent of territory and in the number of its vassals. The towns of Noxcacab, Kabah, Bocal and Nŏhpat were among its dependencies.

The city of Uxmal was founded in 864 AD, according to Maya dating. It was during this period that great avenues paved with stone started being constructed and laid out. The most remarkable of these extends from the interior of the Maya area to the shores of the sea opposite of Cozumel. There were stone paved roads that led to Izamal which were constructed specifically for the convenience of pilgrims.

This was during a time when a long peace existed between the reigning princes of the several linked principal cities. The peace was eventually brought to an end when an alliance formed against the King of Mayapan.

The rulers of Chichen and Uxmal dared to openly condemn the conduct of the king of Mayapan, whose tyrannical exactions forced him to hire bodyguards to protect himself from his own people. He moved to Kimpech, upon which he bestowed upon himself the entire town and its neighborhood as his residence alone. All the inhabitants were now his servants whose royal favors were to serve him.

His people were especially outraged by the introduction of slavery, which had been previously unknown to them. The alliance managed to unseat him, but a change of rulers at Mayapan failed to settle the troubles within the Snake empire. So a conspiracy formed of independent princes and the new tyrant of Mayapan was deposed of after finally being defeated in a three day battle inside the city of Mayapan. The palace was taken and the king and his family were brutally murdered. The city was then put to flames and was left a vast and desolate heap of ruins.

One of the Tutul-Xius princes of Uxmal was then crowned with the title of supreme monarch of the Maya upon his return from vanquishing the second tyrant king.

This new king governed the country with great wisdom and extended his protection over the foreign mercenaries of the former tyrant. He offered them a place of asylum not far from his city of Uxmal. These areas are now the remains of the towns Pockboc, Sakbache and Lebna. During this time the city of Mayapan was then rebuilt and existed to a lesser extent of its former greatness.

Unfortunately, the city of Mayapan was later again the cause of dissension within the Snake kingdom and in 1464 AD was once again destroyed. After its destruction, a peace settled in the Yucatan for more than twenty years. It was during this period of time that there was great abundance and prosperity. At the end of this time, the country was subjected to a series of disasters. Hurricanes came and reaped incalculable damage upon the cities. The population was hit by plagues that brought great destruction of life. This was the beginning of the rapid depopulation of the peninsula. It wasn't but shortly after these great natural disasters and plagues that the Spaniards arrived. The existence of Mesoamerican power in Yucatan came to an end at this point.[90]

The Maya late Classic period during the years 600 through to 900 AD was the high point of Maya culture. Their art, culture, and religion reached their peaks and influenced cultures around them. They had powerful city-states like Tikal and Calakmul that dominated the regions around them. They were much like the Greek city-states, in that the Maya city-states also warred with each other. Occasionally they were allied and traded with one another. There may have been as many as eighty Maya city-states during this time. The cities were controlled by an elite ruling class and their priests whom claimed to be directly descended from the Sun, Moon, stars, and planets.

The cities were holding more people than they could support. Trade for food as well as luxury items was brisk and steadily fed into the center markets. Much as the dilemma that had fallen upon the Romans in their great cities, there became a need to pacify the masses. Public rituals became the norm and ceremonial games came about. The ceremonial ball game became a major feature of all Maya cities.

It was during the Classic period that the ancient Maya ballgame called 'pitz' or 'pok-ta-pok' came around. This ballgame was a very important part of Maya political, religious and social life.

An illustration showing the sacred Maya ball game being played.[226]

The game was played with a rubber ball ranged in size from being as small as a softball to as big as a soccer ball. The game was played with two teams that would attempt to score by bouncing the rubber ball through stone hoops attached to the sides of the ball court. The players could only use their bodies and had to bounce the ball without using their hands

The ball court itself was a focal point of Maya cities and symbolized the city's wealth and power based upon its size and grandeur. The prestige of a city's ball court became as important to the Maya as were their pyramids and temples. They built grand ball courts to hold the games in great public ritual with all the splendor the city had to offer.

Illustration of the Ball Court at Copán, Honduras.[234]

The Mesoamerican ball game is estimated to have been played by many pre-Columbian civilizations in Mesoamerica for over 3,600 years. The ball game was considered a sport, but it was mainly a ritual that was conducted to please the gods. The Maya ball game pok-ta-pok was also played by the Aztec in Mexico, where it was called 'tlachtli.'

Tlachtli was the ball game witnessed being played by Spanish conquistadors whom would later describe in their journals. The ball game was very popular with the people in Mesoamerica. The ball game called batey was played by the islanders of the Greater Antilles. The game played by rubber balls is known to have reached as far south as modern day Paraguay and as far north as to the current state of Arizona.

With the game being played in Mesoamerica for over 3,600 years, it is inevitable that local variations would appear as the game spread to different cultures. The ball game seen by the conquistadors in the 16th century would certainly have differed in several ways from the games that were played much earlier when the game started.

The ball in front of the goal during a Maya game of pok-ta-pok.[275]

Pre-Columbian ball courts have been found throughout Mesoamerica. These ball courts varied considerably in size depending on the size of the city that built them. Regardless of size, they all were built with long narrow alleys that had inward sloped side-walls where the balls could bounce. They also all had stone rings hanging high on the walls for the balls to be bounced through.

The Great Ball Court located in the city of Chichén Itzá is the largest one ever found in all of Mesoamerica. This ball court had an I-shaped playing ground that was 150 meters long with a small temple located at each end.

The ball court, called poctapoc, was very elaborated decorated. There are relief carvings on the lower walls of the ball court depicting ball game activities and ritual sacrifice. At each end of the ball court were small decorated temples and the Temple of the Bearded Man was in front of the court. Another great mystery of the Maya was the temples and carving of 'the bearded man,' as Mesoamericans did not have facial hair.

Sculpture in the Temple of the Warriors at Chichén Itzá.[74]

The acoustics of this structure allow a person standing at one end of the court to be speaking in a natural voice to be heard by another person standing about 150 yards away at the other end of the ball court.

It is not specifically known how the Maya ball game was played, but according to the most widespread version of it, the goal of the game was to pass the ball through one of the rings without touching it. The rules were that the players needed to strike the ball with their hips.

At the Great Ball Court located in Chichén Itzá, they used a solid rubber ball that was about 20 inches in diameter and weighed about 9 lbs or more. It was extremely difficult to get the ball through a ring. In fact, when a player managed to get the ball through the hoop, the game ended with the scored point. The game or possibly the round ended when the ball touched the ground.

The ball game was often played for recreational sport, but major formal ball games were held as ritual events that often featured human sacrifice. There was a high ritual importance behind the Maya ball game of pok-ta-pok. It was a formal religious ceremony that involved the participation of not only religious leaders, but nobility and other important officials. They sang sacred songs and preformed ceremonial dances at these events.

The game was played by two opposing teams, one team was shadow and the other was light. It is believed that the game's winners were given a great feast and hailed as heroes. The losers did not have it as well, as the penalty for losing a game was death. The captain of the losing team was sacrificed It is believed that the sacrificed captain would have a place of honor within the neighboring structure in the Temple of Warriors.

The Maya believed that human sacrifice was necessary for obtaining continued success in agriculture, trade and general health. If the gods did not get human blood to quench their thirst, then they punished the population and in some cases, would destroy the World.[274]

The Maya civilization began to wane towards the end of the Classic period. Nobody knows exactly why, but it has been a continuing mystery to archaeologists for hundreds of years. Around the year 800 AD, the once thriving Maya civilization of Mesoamerica began to rapidly collapse. There were a series of catastrophic volcanic eruptions that had devastated the countryside. This was followed by two extreme droughts that lasted for long periods of time. This goes without mentioning the unending wars that occurred between city-states.

There is evidence of erosion in soils going up slopes. This tells us that farmers had to spread to steeper ground with less suitable soils. Maya agricultural demands did cause substantial erosion of their usable soil. This loss could eventually have undercut their ability to grow enough food to meet their population's demand.[240]

The cities in the highlands were the first to be abandoned. This was an area where for over 16 centuries, the Itza Maya farmers were able to produce an abundance of food on mountainside terraces. It was from their ability to produce an abundance of agricultural surpluses that the great cities in the Maya Lowlands and in the Yucatan

Peninsula were able to grow so large and prosperous.

With the combination of natural disasters, such as volcanic eruptions and hurricanes, the addition of wars and then drought eradicated the abundance of food. The densely populated Maya lowlands were now stricken with famine. This caused more wars and greater starvation so that within the period of a century, most of the cities became abandoned.

Some of the cities in the far north were taken over by the Itza Maya and these city-states continued to thrive for two more centuries. The city of Tikal became an urban center of great importance for the late classic Maya. Some of the landscaping and engineering feats in this city include the largest ancient dam that was ever built by the Maya.

Veneer stones belonging to an ancient Maya dam.[243]

The dam was constructed using a combination of cut stone, rubble and earth. The dam stretched in length for more than 260 feet and held about 20 million gallons of water in a human-made reservoir with 33 foot high walls.

There were periods of excessive rainfall that coincided with a rise in population from 300 to 660 AD. The Maya had to learn to conserve and use their natural resources wisely in order to support a very populous and highly complex society despite the many environmental challenges, which included periodic droughts.[241]

Large-scale alterations in the landscape plus the high demands placed on resources from an ecosystem that caused an extreme amount of stress on environmental conditions. This caused the ever growing harsher conditions to become amplified by increasing amount of climatic aridity developing.

These events made economic and environmental conditions quickly change which caused an increasing amount of social conflict in the region. A climate reversal occurred and a drying trend began to take place at around 660 AD. These adverse conditions triggered political competition and increased warfare. By 1000 AD, the overall sociopolitical instability finally pushed to the Maya elite to diminish control of the cities and migrate elsewhere in the peninsular region. They could not meet the high costs of maintaining the cities with an environment that could no longer sustain the human demand.

Even the flow of commerce had shifted from crossing

the peninsula over land and through the wastelands to moving by sea to go around and avoid it. After the central Maya lowlands were finally abandoned, the environment began to largely recover. However, the Maya population never fully recovered after this period.[242]

This was followed by another extended drought that happened between 1020 to 1100 AD. This drought likely caused huge crop failures that resulted in a famine that caused many deaths. More mass migration out of the areas was ultimately the collapse of the Maya population before the arrival of the Spanish.[244]

Hurricanes have played a key role in much of the devastation that has taken place throughout history of Belize and the Yucatan peninsula. The 'Maya Area' has long been hit with large, devastating hurricanes and tropical storms.

In modern history, a hurricane in 1931 destroyed over two-thirds of the buildings in Belize City and more than 1,000 people had died in that storm. In 1955, 'Hurricane Janet' leveled the northern town of Corozal, Belize. It was only six years later when they were still recovering and rebuilding when "Hurricane Hattie" struck the central coastal area. This hurricane struck the countryside with 300-kph winds and storm tides that were over four meters high.

The devastation of Belize City for the second time in thirty years prompted the relocation of the Belizean capital to be moved 50 miles inland to the planned city of Belmopan. Relocating cities and resettling survivors had occurred several times with the ancient Maya as a result of some of the violent hurricanes they'd experienced.

In 1978, 'Hurricane Greta' hit along the southern coast and then 'Hurricane Iris' made landfall on October 9, 2001. This was a category 4 storm with 145 mph winds that had demolished most of the homes in a village and destroyed the banana crop. It was these kinds of storms that hit the ancient Maya and destroyed their homes and crops. This explains why some regions in the Maya area were periodically abandoned.

In 2007, the category 5 hurricane 'Dean' made landfall north of the Belize/Mexico border and caused extensive damage in northern Belize. Then just three years later, a category 2 level hurricane made landfall approximately 20 miles south-southeast of Belize City on October 25, 2010. That hurricane caused millions of dollars of damage to many crops and buildings.

These modern examples of hurricanes wiping out entire regions would have had an even heavier affect on the Maya, whom if there were any survivors, would have had to abandon the area because all their crops, food stores, possessions, buildings, and any form of livelihood they had would have been completely wiped out.

Areas that would have been wiped out and cleared by hurricane storms, would have been quickly reclaimed by the jungle. This explains why there were reports made by exploring Spaniards of finding regularly overgrown and abandoned Maya cities. These reports were from the first Europeans entering the area. They explain the hardships that they'd endured from storms, including many shipwrecks that resulted from these storms. The often very extreme weather explains the lack of population densities in the Maya area and why there wasn't any real long term success of anything that was man-made in the region.

Chapter 9

The Post-Classic Period (900 AD - 1697 AD)

The Post-Classic Period is the time between the year 900 AD and the conquest of Mesoamerica by the Spaniards between 1521 and 1697 AD. The Post-Classic era was a period in Maya history where military activity became of great importance in order to meet the drastically changing political climate. It was during this time that the political elites were once associated with the priestly class had been relieved of power by groups of warriors.

During the Post-Classic period, at least a half century before the arrival of the Spaniards, the Maya warrior class had yielded its positions of privilege to a very powerful group that were unconnected to the nobility called the "Pochtecas." The Pochtecas were merchants whom had obtained great political power through their economic power. Similar of the modern age, where entities of vast acquired wealth and influence are able to place themselves into positions of power and control. This is what the Pochtecas had done.

These merchants of the Post-Classic period had possessed substantial amounts of wealth and commodities. It was during times of great need and desperation that these wealthy merchants were easily able to seat themselves as rulers. When a current ruling noble house has fallen or lost its influence over the local population, the Pochtecas were swift to move in.

The early part of the Post-Classic period was a period of time characterized by Toltec influence whom had their capital in Tula featuring the Pyramid of Quetzalcoatl, the great shrine to the feathered serpent god. The Toltecs were just north of the Maya and had quickly grown in power and influence. They dominated and influenced much of Mesoamerica until the late 12th century when they fell from power.

The late Post-Classic period begins during the late 12th century, after the Toltec were gone and the Chichimec people began to arrive. These people were linguistically related to the Toltecs and to the Mexica people. They'd begun moving into Mesoamerica and encroaching upon the Maya, whom themselves were already being pushed north because of the changed environment.

These migratory movements by northern people were the result of not just the environment, but of the many social changes that took place during the final period of Mesoamerican civilization. These people came from the northern regions of Mesoamerica were driven by climate changes that threatened their own survival. These migrations from the north caused displacement of many people whom were already permanently settled in the area. Cultures that had been firmly rooted in parts of Mesoamerica for centuries. These newcomers from the north were also bringing their religion and culture with them. These changes had profound influences on the Maya and other Mesoamericans.

There were many cultural changes that took place during the post-classic period. One of them was the introduction and spread of knowledge about metallurgy. Metallurgy was introduced to the Maya sometime at around 800 AD. This knowledge was actually imported from South American cultures whom had already been experimenting with metals.

The Maya did not achieve great expertise with the use of metals. Metal had been occasionally used to make a few trinket items, but wasn't experimented with in general. Most Mesoamericans limited their use of metals to creating jewelry and some tools. New alloys and techniques had been developed in a few centuries later, but metal had little use or value to them.

The most advanced techniques of Mesoamerican metallurgy were developed by the Mixtecos, whom had been influenced by northern cultures. They produced many exquisite handcrafted items from metal, especially that of fine jewelry. Gem setting was one of the Mesoamerican popular uses of metal.

Metal took on a slow role in development in Mesoamerica. It wasn't until later when they began using metals with construction, such as using nails to secure parts of buildings. There were great improvements in mortar and its usage, which allowed for improved construction methods. The Maya began using support columns in their buildings and stone roofs became commonplace in the progressive Maya areas in the post classic period.

Their system of agricultural irrigation became more and more complex to meet their population's demand. In the valley of Mexico, 'chinampas' were used to grow food.

Depiction of Chinampas.[286]

Chinampas were made by using creating small rectangular areas on shallow lake beds and putting fertile arable soil on top to grow crops. They used small rafts to pole their way between them. This method was used extensively in the valley of Mexico by the Mexica people to grow a majority of their food. The Mexica had built over 200,000 chinampas around their city to meet their agricultural needs.

The political system throughout Mesoamerica had undergone major changes during the early Post-Classic period. Many warlike political elites were now legitimizing their positions by means of a strict adherence to a complex set of religious beliefs they had learned from the Toltec culture.[155] According to this system, the ruling classes proclaimed themselves to being the direct descendants of the god Quetzalcoatl. They had an entire priest class back their claims of lineage to highly revered. The Plumed Serpent, Quetzalcoatl was one of the creative forces of the universe and also a cultural hero in Mesoamerican mythology and culture. Being able to claim lineage to this god gave the ruler unquestionable right to reign.

These new rulers also declared themselves to be the heirs of a mythical city of the gods called, "Zuyuá" in Mayan. Another feature of the newly adopted religious system was that it allowed the formation of alliances with other city-states that were controlled by groups that had the same ideology.

This was the case with the League of Mayapán in Yucatán. These northern Maya and neighboring cultures had united under religion. This was same with the Mixtec confederation of Lord Eight Deer, based north of the Maya in the mountains of Oaxaca. At this point in the Post-Classic period, many Mesoamerican societies can be characterized by their military nature and multi-ethnic populations.

The fall of Tula and the militaristic Toltec checked the power in the new religious system. The alliances broke down with the dissolution of the League of Mayapán. The Mixtec state unification fell apart as well the abandonment of religious leadership coming from Tula.

Mesoamerica was now receiving new immigrants from northern regions. These groups of people from the north were related to the ancient Toltecs, but had completely different ideologies than the existing residents. The final arrivals to the Mesoamerican region before the coming of the Spanish were the Mexica. They'd established themselves on a small island on Lake Texcoco under the dominion of the Texpanecs of Azcapotzalco.

The Mexica arrived and settled, then later conquered a large part of Mesoamerica They then created a unified and centralized state. A centralized empire whose only rivals were the Tarascan state of Michoacán. Neither one of these people could defeat each other in warfare. Both had tried to defeat the other several times. The military stalemate led the way to creating a loose non-aggression pact between the two people.

When the Spaniards arrived in Mesoamerica, many of the people that were controlled by the Mexica, no longer wished to remain under their rule. They seen the arrival of the conquering Spaniards as an opportunity to free themselves and agreed to support the Europeans in their conquest against the Mexica. They thought that in return for helping the Spanish that they'd gain their freedom. They had no idea that they were assisting in the entire subjugation of all the Mesoamerican world by the European newcomers.

The Post-Classic Era saw the collapse of many of the great Mesoamerican nations and Maya city-states that had dominated the region during the Classic Era. Not all of them had perished during the post classic period before the arrival of the Spanish. The Maya of the Yucatán continued to exist as a distinct culture and in many cases their great cities at Chichen Itza and Uxmal thrived. However, this was a period of increased social chaos and warfare.

The Post-Classic was a time of technological advancement in architecture, engineering and weaponry, but it was also a period of cultural decline. However, it was during the Post-Classic period that Mesoamerica experienced rapid movements and growths in population, this was especially true in Central Mexico after 1200 AD. It was also a time of experimentation in governance.

For example, in Yucatán, 'dual rulership' apparently replaced the more theocratic governments of Classic times. Post classic era seen oligarchic councils controlled by the few elite now controlled much of Central Mexico. The wealthy 'pochteca' merchants backed by military orders had become more powerful than they were during the Classic period. This afforded some Mesoamericans a degree of social mobility that would have otherwise never presented it's self.

By the 1400's, there was a renewal of Maya populations spreading in Southern Yucatán and Guatemala. There was a renaissance of fine arts and science as the culture flourished. Just north of the regrowing Maya was the Aztec Empire that had risen to power in the early 15th century.

The Aztec were on a fast path to exerting their dominance over the entire Mexico valley region until Mesoamerica had been discovered by Spanish explorers. The Post Preclassic period ended shortly after the discovery and the arrival of Spanish conquistadors. The start of the 16th century would have a profound impact on the entirety of Mesoamerica to the point of extinction of many native cultures.

In 1492, Christopher Columbus sailed across the ocean and discovered the Bahamas. He named and claimed these islands 'San Salvador,' on behalf of the Kingdom of Spain (Castile and Leon). He encountered an indigenous people on the islands, whom were peaceful and friendly. He spoke of them in his journal.

On October 12, 1492, Christopher Columbus wrote:

"Many of the men I have seen have scars on their bodies, and when I made signs to them to find out how this happened, they indicated that people from other nearby islands come to San Salvador to capture them; they defend themselves the best they can. I believe that people from the mainland come here to take them as slaves. They ought to make good and skilled servants, for they repeat very quickly whatever we say to them. I think they can very easily be made Christians, for they seem to have no religion. If it pleases our Lord, I will take six of them to Your Highnesses when I depart, in order that they may learn our language."[85]

Columbus also remarked that their lack of modern weaponry and tactical vulnerability in writing:

"I could conquer the whole of them with 50 men, and govern them as I pleased."[86]

Columbus also explored the northeast coast of Cuba, where he landed and also claimed for Spain on October 28, 1492. It was during Columbus' second voyage in 1494, that he passed along the southern coast of the Cuban island and landed at various inlets including what was later to become Guantanamo Bay.

After receiving news of the discoveries upon Columbus' return, King Ferdinand and Queen Isabella of Spain urged Pope Alexander VI to confirm their right of possession to all of the newly discovered lands in the Americas. The Pope was persuaded and in the Papal Bull of 1493, known as the Doctrine of Discovery, Pope Alexander VI commanded Spain to conquer, colonize and convert the pagans in the New World to Catholicism.[87][88]

Private adventurers and investors scrambled to enter into contracts with the Spanish Crown in order to conquer the newly discovered lands in return for tax revenues and the power to rule.[60] The Spanish had quickly colonized the Caribbean and established their center of operations on the island of Cuba within the first decades after the initial discovery of the New World.

The Spanish heard rumors of a rich empire to the west belonging to the Aztec on the mainland of the New World. Hernán Cortés then set sail the coast of Mexico with eleven ships in 1519 to seek out this rich empire of the Aztec. By August 1521, the Aztec empire had fallen and their capital of Tenochtitlan was conquered by the Spanish. Then within a three year period after the fall of the Aztec capital, the Spanish had conquered a large part of Mexico.

This newly conquered Mesoamerican territory became New Spain, known as the Viceroyalty of New Spain, from 1521 until the end of Spanish control in 1821. New Spain was governed by a viceroy whom only answered to the King of Spain through of the Spanish Empire's Royal and Supreme Council of the Indies.

Further desiring to expand conquered territory, Cortés dispatched Pedro de Alvarado with an army to conquer the Mesoamerican kingdoms in the Guatemalan Sierra Madre and neighboring Pacific plain. This was the military phase of the establishment of the Spanish colony of Guatemala which lasted from 1524 to 1541.[61]

When the colony was formed, the Captaincy General of Guatemala established its capital at Santiago de los Caballeros de Guatemala. This colony governed a wide territory that included the modern day Mexican state of Chiapas, and the modern nations of El Salvador, Honduras and Costa Rica.[62] The Spanish had imposed strict colonial rule over the Yucatán region from 1527 to 1546 . They had later gained control over Verapaz and ruled it from the 16th to 17th centuries. They left the area between Petén and most of Belize independent long after the surrounding people had been subjugated.[63]

Bernal Díaz del Castillo was the chronicler who gave the most detail about the voyage of Hernández de Córdoba. Bernal dates March 4, 1517 as the first encounter with the indigenous people of the Yucatán Saying the Spaniards asked the natives for the name of the land they'd just arrived upon and the natives replied in their language saying, "Tectetán," which means, "I don't understand you." The Spaniards did not understand what the natives were saying, so took their word Tectetán and mispronounced it, 'Yucatán' as being the name of the land.[92] The same happened with a cape made by the land there. When inquiring about the structures the Spaniards spotted, the natives responded with, "Catoche," meaning "our houses." The Spanish mistook this for the name of the settlement and the cape where they had arrived.

Chapter 10

The Spanish Conquest of the Maya.

First contact between the Spanish and the Maya occurred in the year 1511. This was 19 years after Columbus discovered the Bahamas in 1492. The first contact between the Spanish and the Maya occurred after a shipwreck had brought the survivors to Maya shores. The written account of the shipwreck and of the events that followed are written in Bernal Díaz's, "Verdadera Historia de la Conquista de Nueva España" (in english: True History of the Conquest of New Spain).[50]

Many of the details written by Díaz differ than the accounts given from other 16th century chroniclers, such as Cervantes, Gómara, and Martyr. All of whom differ in their accounts of the number aboard the ship, how many survivors had reached the shore, and the ultimate fate of said survivors. They do, however, all agree that ultimately at least two of them had survived the shipwreck and the events that followed.

The first known Spanish landing on the Yucatán

Peninsula and first contact with the Maya was the result of a catastrophe happening at sea. A small ship from Darién Panama sailing to Santo Domingo on Hispaniola had run aground on some shoals in the Caribbean Sea just south of the island of Jamaica in 1511.[51] There were fifteen men and two women aboard this damaged ship. They abandoned ship and attempted to set off in the ship's boat to try to reach Hispaniola or one of the other Spanish colonies.

Their attempts to reach any Spanish colonies failed when prevailing currents carried them westwards. The ship survivors drifted helplessly with the current for two weeks. Eventually the current carried them to land, where they arrived somewhere on the eastern shoreline of the Yucatán Peninsula. The exact location of their landing is not known, but it could have possibly been somewhere along the coast of present-day Belize.[52]

The shipwreck survivors made it to land and were swiftly captured by some local Maya and were then divided up as slaves among several of the chieftains. A number of the surviving Spanish shipwreck crew were also sacrificed according to customary Maya offertory practices.[53]

Over the following years their numbers began to dwindle when some died from disease or because of exhaustion from being overworked. Eventually there were only two men left. The two remaining survivors were Gerónimo de Aguilar and Gonzalo Guerrero. Aguilar had managed to escape from his captor and found refuge with another Maya ruler. Gonzalo Guerrero managed to win over some prestige among the Maya for his bravery.

Guerrero achieved the standing of a ranking Maya warrior and granted the status of a noble.

These two men would later play two very different roles in future conflicts between the Spanish and the Maya people. Gerónimo de Aguilar would become Hernán Cortés' Mayan translator and an adviser in assisting Spain conquer the Maya states. Gonzalo Guerrero would remain with the Maya people, serving as a tactician and as a warrior fighting with them against the Spanish.

The next contact between the Spaniards and the Maya happened in the year 1517, when the Spanish conquistador Francisco Hernández de Córdoba sailed to the Yucatán from Cuba in search of slaves to replace the native Cuban slaves that were dying off in great numbers. The Spaniards were surprised to see stone cities along the coast of Yucatán. Córdoba and his men landed at several locations. Some of the Maya greeted the Spaniards with friendship and offered to trade goods with them. The Spaniards were lucky to acquire a few pieces of gold ornaments by trading.

However, the Spaniards weren't always friendly greeted by the Maya, such as the incident at Cape Cotoche when the explorers landed at the coast to gather fresh water inland. Córboda and his men were ambushed with about 80 Spaniards being wounded by a volley of stones, arrows, and darts. The Spanish quickly learned that even though the Maya arrows weren't attaining any distinct force behind them, they still tended to shatter on impact which lead to a slow and painful death.

Ultimately, the Spaniards had failed in their attempts to

gather water and repair their water casks. Córdoba was forced to redistribute the remaining of his men on other ships and abandon his smallest ship, a brigantine which had paid for on credit.[54]

The expedition returned to Cuba to report on the discovery of this new land and of the incident at the Cape. Diego Velázquez, whom was governor of Cuba, ordered four ships out on an expedition of 240 men to this land. They were supplied with crossbows, muskets, salt pork, and cassava bread . The expedition was led by his nephew, Juan de Grijalva.[55] The Grijalva expedition experienced similar relations with the native Maya, some were friendly and some being hostile. Grijalva was genuinely anxious to fulfill Velázquez' order to explore the new lands rather than conquer.

Except for occasionally firing a few cannon shots out of spite, Grijalva repeatedly denied himself and his men the gratification of vengeance from periodic attacks they received from some Maya as they sailed along the coast of the Yucatán for months. Occasionally a friendly group would exchange beads and Spanish wine for food and other necessities the expedition required. Grijalva was disappointed at the fact that they'd gathered very little gold on their trip; but when they came back to Cuba he shared a tale of hearing about a rich empire that was further to the west inland.

This story prompted Hernán Cortés to lead an expedition into the Yucatán in 1519. Cortés had spent some time at the island of Cozumel off the coast of the Yucatán where he tried to convert the locals to Christianity, but had limited and mixed results. This was when he'd heard the rumors of other 'bearded white men' that were living in the area. Cortés sent messengers to these 'bearded white men' whom turned out to be Gerónimo de Aguilar and Gonzalo Guerrero, the last two survivors of the 1511 shipwreck. Upon receiving Cortés message, Aguilar petitioned his Maya chieftain to be allowed to leave and join his former countrymen. The Chieftain agreed to release him and Aguilar made his way to where Cortés and his men's ships were located.

Gerónimo de Aguilar claimed that he tried to convince Guerrero to leave with him, but failed. Guerrero was now already well-assimilated into the Maya culture and was looked upon as a figure of rank by the local Maya. Aguilar claimed that Guerrero had a Maya wife and three children at the Maya settlement of Chetumal where he was now living.[56]

Aguilar would prove himself to be a valuable asset as a translator for Cortés expedition into the Yucatán. He had lived with the Maya for so long that he was now quite fluent in speaking "Yucatec Mayan," along with a few other local indigenous languages.[57]

Gonzalo Guerrero's fate was never known. It is assumed that for some years that he fought alongside the Maya warriors against the Spanish Conquistadors. He provided the Maya with military counsel on tactics to fight and resist the Spanish invasion. Although unconfirmed, Guerrero is believed to have later been killed in a battle.

However, Hernán Cortés and some 500 Conquistadors were currently engaged in the richer lands of Mexico. The quest for gold kept the attention of the Spaniards in the Mexico region for a few years. By 1511, the Spanish Conquistadors led by Cortés had defeated the mighty Aztec Empire with the use of modern weapons and the assistance of thousands of Mesoamerican allies.

It was the Spanish Conquistador Pedro de Alvarado whom was granted the privilege of conquering the Maya after he and his brothers had proven themselves in the ranks of Cortes' army. In the year 1523, he set out with approximately four hundred Spanish Conquistadors and about ten-thousand Mesoamerican allies to conquer the Maya.

By the year 1524, Pedro de Alvarado's band of Spanish Conquistadors and his native allies moved into the Maya area which is now present-day Guatemala. The Maya civilization had already deteriorated some centuries before the arrival of the Spanish. Only a number of small kingdoms remained of the once populous Maya city-states.

The strongest of the remaining Maya kingdoms was the kingdom of the K'iche. These people were located in the area that is now central Guatemala. The K'iche people had rallied around a leader named Tecún Umán to defend their lands and met Alvarado's Conquistadors and indigenous allies in battle. Unfortunately, the K'iche lost the battle and were permanently defeated, ending any significant native resistance in the area.

Another Spanish conquistador, Francisco de Montejo

had also joined Hernán Cortés in the conquest of Mexico. In 1526, Montejo had successfully petitioned the King of Spain for the right to conquer the Maya of Yucatán. He arrived in eastern Yucatán in 1527 and was at first greeted peaceably by the local Maya. Of the first few settlements that the Spanish encountered, most local chiefs agreed to the Conquistador's demands that they swear oaths of loyalty to the King of Spain. The chieftains agreed because they'd heard news of the Spanish conquest of the Aztecs.

However, as the Spanish advanced further into Maya territory, they found entire cities that were already deserted when they reached them. As the Spanish progressed deeper into the Maya area, they started getting harassed. When they traveled inland even further, they began being openly attacked.

Montejo had his men set up a small fort on the Yucatán coast at 'Xaman Ha' in 1528, but they were unsuccessful in subduing the country and maintain their position. Montejo moved his conquistadors on to Mexico and subdued Tabasco in 1530.

Montejo returned to the Yucatán peninsula in 1531 with a force of conquistadors that were allied with the Maya port city of Campeche.[58] While he set up a fortress in Campeche to base his campaign, he sent his son, Francisco Montejo the Younger (el Mozo), inland with an army to conquer the Maya. As the Conquistador army made their way inland, the leaders of some Maya states pledged that they'd be Spanish allies. Montejo the Younger continued on to Chichen Itza, which he conquered and then declared as the royal capital of the Spanish Yucatán. Only a few months later the locals started to rise up against the Spaniards. The conquistadors were now being constantly attacked, forcing them to eventually flee to Honduras.

It was rumored that Gonzalo Guerrero, the shipwrecked Spaniard that had assimilated with the Maya, was among the Maya warriors helping direct their resistance against the Spanish. Meanwhile, at the fort in Campeche, the elder Montejo was also being frequently besieged and the morale of his men were plummeting. Many of the conquistadors led by the elder Montejo were tired of a long fight with nothing to show for it. They stated that they desired to find easier and more profitable conquests elsewhere.

Meanwhile, the younger Montejo continued to fight the Maya that were becoming more hostile as their numbers grew. They eventually they laid siege to the Spanish barricaded in the city. The Maya were able to cut off the Spanish supply line to the coast and forced them to send for help as they barricaded themselves in the ruins of the ancient city of Chichén Itzá.

Months passed, but no reinforcements came to the aid of the trapped Spaniards. Montejo the Younger attempted an all out assault against the Maya to break their siege and lost 150 of his few remaining forces. He was forced to abandon the city of Chichén Itzá under cover of darkness in 1534.

By the year 1535, Montejo was forced to withdraw his forces to Veracruz and leave the Yucatán once again completely in the control of the Maya. At this point, Francisco de Montejo's men were exhausted, demoralized, and having found no loot after all their efforts, his conquistadors deserted him.

In the year 1540, Montejo, whom has now aged into his late 60's, passed over his rights to conquer the Yucatán by the King of Spain over to his son, Francisco Montejo the Younger. His son immediately renewed the conquest of the Maya and invaded the Yucatán with a renewed large force. By the year 1542, Montejo the Younger had effectively subdued the Western portion of the Yucatán peninsula and then placed his capital in the Maya city of T'ho, which he renamed to Mérida.

The conquered Maya lord of the Tutul Xiu Maya converted to Christianity and swore an oath of loyalty to the King of Spain. The Tutul Xiues had dominated most of the western Yucatán. They became valuable allies to the Spanish, especially against their enemy the Cocom Maya. The Spaniards were in great need of assistance with conquering the rest of the peninsula, as was proven by previous attempts.

The conquest against the Maya in the eastern portion of the Yucatán peninsula came to an end in 1546. With the assistance of the Tutul Xiu, the Spanish defeated a final combined army of mixed forces from the last remaining Maya states in the eastern Yucatán peninsula.

There were a number of Maya states that had pledged loyalty to Spain at first, but they'd later revolt after feeling the heavy hand of Spanish rule. The Maya continued to revolt against their oppressive conquerors for years. There were periodic revolts occurred throughout the Spanish

Colonial Era that followed, but they were violently put down by Spanish troops.

The Spanish had unknowingly released a vicious ally ahead of them in their conquest of the New World: disease. The indigenous inhabitants of the New World had no immunity to European diseases such as: smallpox, bubonic plague, chicken pox, mumps and more. These diseases quickly spread through Mesoamerican communities and more than decimated the population.

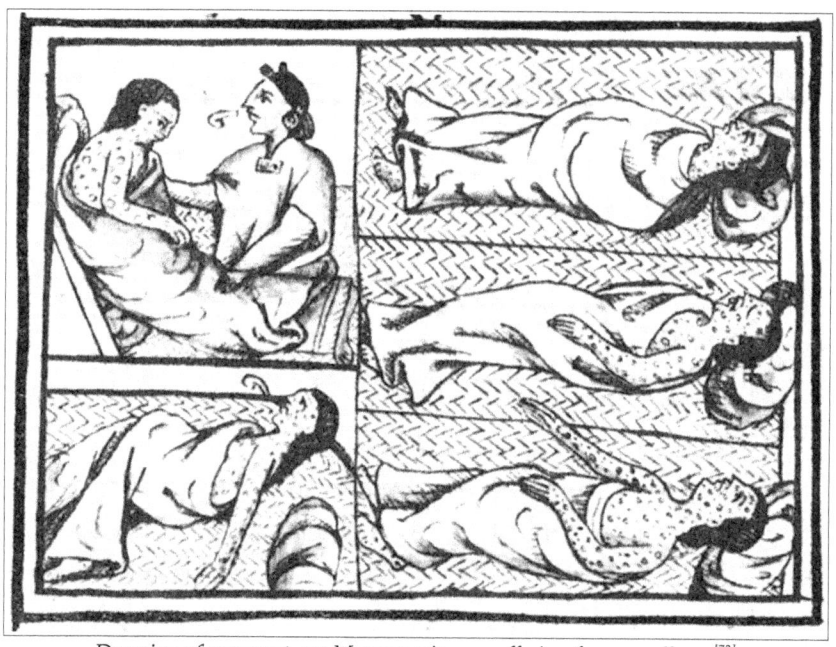

Drawing of conquest-era Mesoamericans suffering from smallpox.[72]

It is estimated that more than a third of the Maya population perished from European carried disease between the years 1521 to 1523. But besides the spread of disease, the Spaniards also had other advantages: horses, guns, war dogs, metal armor, steel swords and crossbows.

All of these were devastating unknown things to Mesoamericans, of which they were not prepared to defend against.

The arrival of the Spanish brought Mesoamericans the combination of disease, war, slavery and forced relocation that nearly wiped them completely out. Their cultures never recovered. It's estimated that about 88% of the Maya inhabitants died during the first decade of Spanish colonial rule due to a combination of disease and war. Although disease was responsible for the majority of deaths, ruthless warfare between rival Maya groups and Spanish expeditions is what pushed the population over the edge.[64]

The Spanish conquest of the Petén Itza Kingdom was the last stage to conquering Guatemala. The Petén Basin is a wide lowland plain that's covered with a dense tropical rain forest that is now part of modern Guatemala. Cortés had visited this region before during his march to Honduras in 1525. The chieftains of the local Itza Maya that he encountered had all pledged their loyalty to Spain to prevent Cortés from attacking them, but was thereafter neglected as soon as the Spanish left their area.

There had been a few small attempts over the years by the Spanish to convert and conquer the Itza Maya, but all failed. For example, in 1622 the Spanish Governor of the Yucatán sent a force of twenty Spaniards and 140 converted Christian Maya allies to march on the Itza capital city of Tayasal, but Itza warriors quickly killed them. A similar force was sent to the Petén Basin in 1624 whom were ambushed by Itza warriors and met the same fate as the previous groups.

Due to other areas needing suppressed by other Maya uprisings, the Governor of Yucatán decided his best use of troops and resources would be better spent elsewhere. The Itza Maya continued their independence harassed for the most part through the 17th century. The Itza Maya of the Petén Basin were the last of the significant unconquered Maya kingdoms.[59] The Itza Maya still had significant population that existed in the Petén Basin with most of them living around the central lakes and along the rivers.

The Maya in the Petén were not politically unified as a whole single kingdom. Instead, they were divided into a number of different complex alliances and old rival enmities that were intermixed with other Maya groups in the area. The most significant groups that were around the Petén central lakes were the Itza, the Yalain and the Kowoj. The other groups whose territories were also in the Petén Basin were the Kejache, Acala, Lacandon, Xocmo, Chinamita, Icaiche and the Manche Ch'ol.

It was late in the 17th century, when the last Itza Maya ruler began to be more open minded towards the Spaniards. He would receive and protect Spanish emissaries at the capital city of Tayasal. In the year 1695, three Franciscans friars headed to Tayasal and they were well received when they arrived. A number of the Itza Maya had even consented to being baptized as Christians. However, the Itza King refused to convert to Christianity and pledge his loyalty to Spain. This provoked the Spanish governor of Yucatán to react by sending a force of sixty

Spanish soldiers accompanied by Maya allies to the Petén Basin the following year. However, as before, the Spaniards were swiftly beaten back by fierce Itza attacks.

This was when the Spanish governor in the city of Mérida decided that a major force needed to be sent. The following year in 1697 the Spanish Basque conquistador Martín de Ursúa y Arizmendi led a force of 235 Spanish conquistadors and tens of thousands of Xiu Maya marched into the Petén Basin. This time they brought along artillery and a large supply train of mules and men to cut a path through the jungle.

The conquistadors set up a fort on the shore of Lake Petén Itza across from the Itza city of Tayasal and from there they reconstructed a small ship on the lake that they had brought with them that had been disassembled in pieces. Then on March 13, 1697, with everything ready and artillery supporting this large force, they defeated the Itza Maya and seized their capital of Tayasal. The Maya conquest had finally ended with the capture of Tayasal, the island capital of the Itza kingdom.

The Spanish didn't stop at conquering the city, they smashed all the idols of false gods and burned all the Itza Maya's books that 'contained lies of the devil.' The conquistadors reported that there were so many idols within the city that it took them nearly all day to smash them all.

Bishop Landa, whom was with the Conquistadors, described the Maya's books as being large and made with a highly decorated leaf that was doubled in folds which were enclosed between two boards. The Maya wrote on both sides in the columns that were corresponding to the book folds. The paper they used to make their books was made from the roots of a tree, which they put a white varnish on to give a nice surface to write upon.

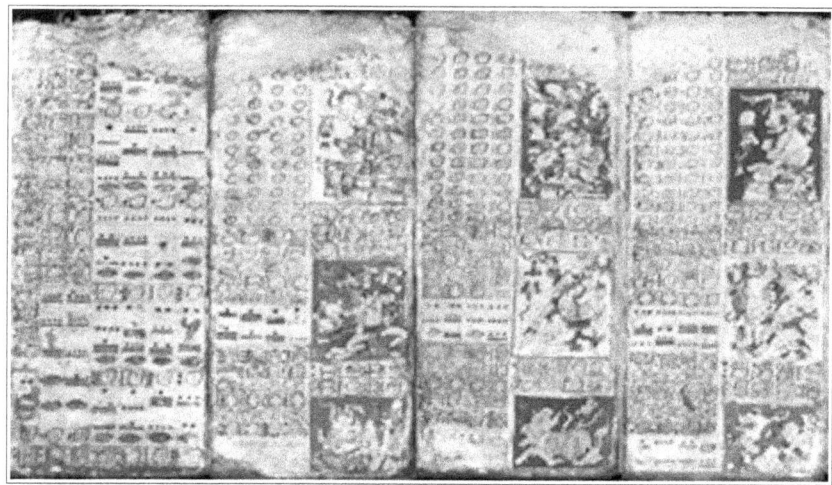

The Dresden Codex, 1 of only 4 Maya books that survived the Spanish Conquest.

This art of writing and bookmaking was only known by certain men of high rank. Because of their knowledge in writing and bookmaking, they were held in much esteem by the people.

These writers did not practice their art in public, but the Maya people understood their writings and the meanings behind the characters that they used. The writers taught them and made them understand their meanings. In these books, these writers wrote about their antiquities, myths and of their sciences.

The Spaniards found a great number of these books among the Maya, they were a common item, However, the

Spanish believed that these books contained nothing but heretic superstitions and falsities from the devil, so to they burned them all.[91]

The Pyramid of Kukulcan seen from the Temple of the Warriors at Chichen-Itza.[75]

Following the Spanish Conquest of Mesoamerica, the Vice-royalty of New Spain (Virreinato de Nueva España), also known as "New Spain," was established. New Spain was a vice-royalty of the crown of Castile, of the Spanish empire, which comprised of territories in the north overseas 'Septentrion' (North America and Philippines).

Within this Septentrion included most of the United States west of the Mississippi River, including the lower gulf coast and all of Florida. Additionally, New Spain included the Caribbean, Mexico and all of Central America excluding Panama.

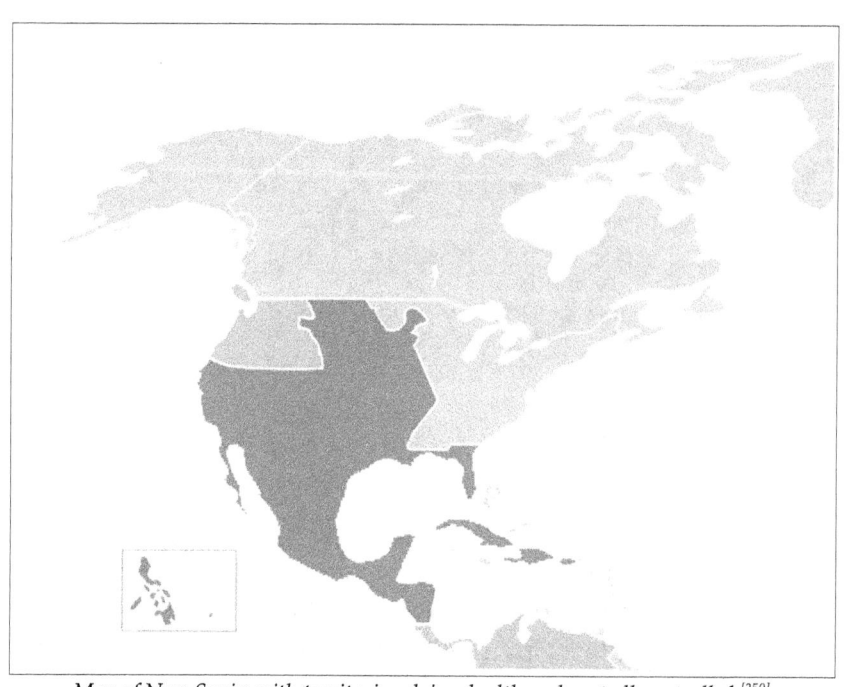
Map of New Spain with territories claimed, although not all controlled.[250]

The Viceroyalty of New Spain's territory included:

- The Bay Islands until 1643
- The Cayman Islands until 1670
- Central America to the southern border of Costa Rica until 1821
- Cuba to 1898
- Florida
- Hispaniola including Haiti until 1697
- Santo Domingo until 1821
- Jamaica until 1655
- Mariana Islands 1898
- Mexico until 1821
- Philippines 1898
- Puerto Rico 1898
- The Southwest United States
- British Columbia and Alaska, redefined by the Adams-Onís Treaty in 1819
- Venezuela until 1739

These territories were separated into provinces that were led by a governor whom was responsible for the province's administration and leading the province's army and local militias. The Spanish provinces were grouped together under five high courts that were called, "Audiencias" at Santo Domingo, Mexico City, Guatemala, Guadalajara and Manila. Both the high courts and the governors had autonomy from the Viceroy and carried out most of their duties on their own. Only on important issues did the Viceroy become involved in ruling the provinces directly.

As Spain's global power weakened, the previous colonies of what was once the Viceroyalty of New Spain, all eventually became independent nations of their own right. Their descendants, combined the cultures of the indigenous population and that of the European cultures that came and settled into their own cultures.

In it's height, the Maya civilization had one of the richest cultures in the New World. Today, there's an estimated 20 to 30 million direct descendants of the ancient Maya civilization that currently reside in southern Mexico, Belize, Honduras, El Salvador and Guatemala.

Part 2

Ancient Maya Ways

Chapter 11

The Maya Calender

The ancient Maya kept track of time differently than how we do today. They used a calendar system which had remarkable accuracy and complexity. It was a calendar system that was utilized and expressed in many forms, including pyramid temples which acted as calenders.

The Pyramid of Kukulkan at Chichén Itzá in Yucatan, Mexico was built around sometime between the years 550 to 900 AD. The earliest hieroglyphic date discovered at Chichen Itza dates to 832 AD, when the Toltec culture from Tula became politically powerful and dominated the region.

The pyramid built there has four stairways for each quarter of the year and each stairwell has 91 steps that lead to a platform at the top. This makes for a total of 365 steps/platforms, the same number of days in a calendar year.

The pyramid also has nine main platforms which are thought to represent the 18 months of the Maya calendar they called the "haab'." Additionally, there are 52 panels on the pyramid which represent, not only the number of weeks, but the number of years that it takes for a calendar round date to recycle. More impressive, on the Spring and Fall Equinoxes of each year, a special occurrence happens with the Pyramid to mark the occasion.

During the Equinox, the Sun projects a waving pattern of light on the northern stairway for a few hours in the late afternoon. This pattern of shadow and light is caused by the angle of the Sun in the sky during the Equinox as it hits the edge of the nine steps of the pyramid's main construction. These triangles of light connect with a massive stone carving of a snake's head at the base of the stairs, giving the impression of a massive serpent snaking down the structure.

The famous decent of the snake god Kukulkan during the Spring Equinox. [280]

Twice a year, when the lengths of day and night are equal, this pyramid dedicated to "Kukulcan" (or "Quetzalcoatl") is visited by the feathered serpent god. On every equinox, "Kukulcan" returns to Earth to commune with his worshipers and provide blessings for a full harvest and good health before entering into the sacred water, where he descends through on his way to the underworld, "Xibalba."

Mesoamericans took their calenders as astronomy serious. Their temples were aligned to meet the needs of a particular god and accurately counted off the days ever year to mark when the god was to be celebrated. The Maya calendar system was also used by the other Mesoamerican nations, such as the Aztecs and the Toltec. They adopted the mechanics of the calendar, but changed the names of the days of the week and the months to meet their language and cultural differences.

The Maya calendar used a system that moved in cycles, with the last cycle ending on our modern date of December 21st, 2012. This is the last day of the Maya calender which corresponds with the Winter Solstice, which occurs on the date of December 21st. This has been the reasoning behind the hype in 2012 about the Maya predicting when the World was coming to an end. This was just a cycle of their calender, which merely mean that the count began again at one.

We're still here, so obviously that wasn't the meaning behind the new cycle of the Maya calendar. The World did not come to an end.

The Maya Long Count Calendar's dates were written out as five hieroglyphs separated by four periods.[15]

The Maya calendar worked in cycles which they called, "B'ak'tun." A Maya calendar's B'ak'tun runs for 144,000 days long per cycle. The thirteenth B'ak'tun on the Maya Calender ended recently on the modern date of December 21, 2012. The following day on December 22 marked the start of the fourteenth B'ak'tun of the Maya calendar. The Maya calender continues its count in these cycles for 'octillions' of years into the distant future.

Octillion (n) - the number that is represented as a one followed by 27 zeros (10^{27}). 1,000,000,000,000,000,000,000,000,000

The Maya Calender consists of three separate corresponding calenders; the Long Count, the Tzolkin (divine calender), and the Haab (civil calender).

The Long Count Date

In Maya dating, the date reads from left to right with the 'Long Count' date coming first, starting with the longest years counts on the left all the way down to the day being marked on the right end, then the 'Tzolkin date' and then lastly, the 'Haab date'. For example, using the Maya calender numbering system, a typical date would read as: "13.0.0.0.0 4 Ahau, 8 Kumku."

- "13.0.0.0.0" is the Long Count calendar date,
- "4 Ahau" is the Tzolkin calendar date, and
- "8 Kumku" is the Haab' calendar date.

Here's how the Long Count date works:

Maya long count dates are written out from left to right with five numbers which are separated by four periods, written as such: 13.0.0.0.0

The year is marked to the far left, with the day being counted to the far right. The ancient Maya represented these number values with their own beautifully designed hieroglyphs instead of using actual numerals, as we are in these examples.

The number on the right-most position is called the "k'in," which counts single days, for example: 13.0.0.0.**1**,

141

13.0.0.0.**2**, 13.0.0.0.**3**, etc.. The Maya counted the days to 20. The "k'in" counts up to 19 and then goes back to zero, with counting picked back up by the next position, called the "uinal" (winals). So counting up from the day 13.0.0.0.**19** would become 13.0.0.**1**.0.

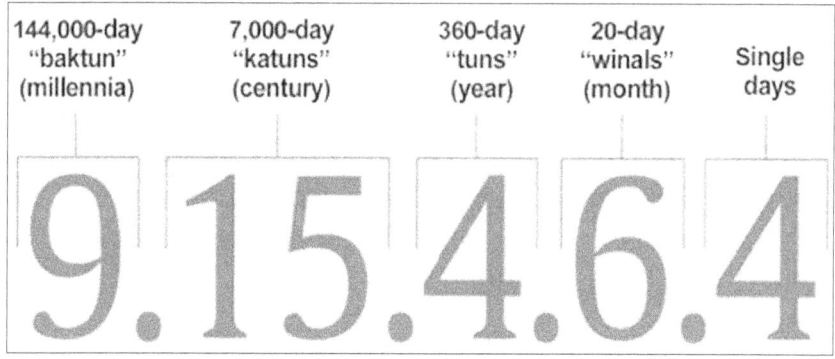

Example of Long Count date by Columbia Pictures[18]

Each "uinal" is a block of 20 days (k'in), equivalent to months. After an 'uinal' is added, the 'k'in' position then picks back up, again counting up to 19 and then adding to the 'uinal' on the 20th count. So the day after 13.0.0.**1**.0 would be 13.0.0.1.**1** and then 13.0.0.1.**2**, all the way up to 13.0.0.1.**19** until finally adding an 'uinal' to make 13.0.0.**2**.0.

The 'uinals' count upward as well. While the Maya generally used a base-20 counting system in everything they did, the Long Count is really a mixed base-20 and base-18 system that represents the number of days since the start of Maya creation of the World. To make this work, they modify this slightly for the 'uinals,' which only counts up to 17 before rolling over at 18 to the third position (middle), which is called the "tun."

Each "tun" is 18 blocks of 20 days, which equals 360

days. A tun is approximately a year by the solar calendar. The 'tuns' in turn count up to 19 and at 20, roll over into the fourth position from the right, which are called, "k'atuns." A k'atun is 20 blocks of 360 days, which adds up to 7,200 days, or just under 20 years. The k'atun counts up to 19, before reaching 20 and rolling over into the final digit of the Long Count, called the "b'ak'tun."

If the word, "b'ak'tun," sounds familiar, it's because on the modern date of December 21, 2012 on our calendar marked the end of the "13th b'ak'tun" of the Maya Long Count Calendar. In other words, it's the day the count will read 13.0.0.0.0. On December 22, 2012 the Maya Long Count Calendar read as 13.0.0.0.1. Each "b'ak'tun" is 144,000 days long, which is just under 400 years. To the ancient Maya, the 13th b'ak'tun represented a full cycle of creation according to their beliefs.

The Maya never made any apocalyptic prophecies about the "End of the World" or anything like that. The Long Count is an astronomical calendar that was used to track long periods of time, which the Maya called the "universal cycle." Each of these cycles are 2,880,000 days long, which is about 7885 solar years. The beginning of the 13th b'ak'tun was on August 11, 3114 BC on the Gregorian calendar or September 6, 3114 BC on the Julian calendar.

This date marks the creation of the World for human beings, according to Maya Mythology. The ancient Maya believed that it was on this "Creation Date" that "Raised-up-Sky-Lord" caused three stones to be set by associated gods at "Lying-Down-Sky, First-Three-Stone-Place."

Because the sky still lay on the primordial sea, it was black, the setting of the three stones centered the cosmos which allowed the sky to be raised and revealed the sun. The creation of the World inhabitable by humans.[282][194][195][196][197][198]

The belief that the end and start of a calendaric cycle is going to trigger some event still inspires a myriad of prophesies about the end of the world. The final episode in the Creation Myth concluded with the creation of humans with no further destruction/recreation cycles. Even though the Maya started their calendar based on their belief of the creation of the World, their calendar was nothing more than a means to record the date and events.

The Maya had the capacity to count millions of years into the future, but rarely used units that were larger than "b'ak'tuns."

Here is a list of the Maya Long Count b'ak'tuns compared to modern dating:

Long Count	Modern Date
0	Mon, Aug 11, 3114 BC
1.0.0.0.0	Thu, Nov 13, 2720 BC
2.0.0.0.0	Sun, Feb 16, 2325 BC
3.0.0.0.0	Wed, May 21, 1931 BC
4.0.0.0.0	Sat, Aug 23, 1537 BC
5.0.0.0.0	Tue, Nov 26, 1143 BC
6.0.0.0.0	Fri, Feb 28, 748 BC
7.0.0.0.0	Mon, Jun 3, 354 BC
8.0.0.0.0	Thu, Sep 5, 41 AD
9.0.0.0.0	Sun, Dec 9, 435 AD
10.0.0.0.0	Wed, Mar 13, 830 AD
11.0.0.0.0	Sat, Jun 15, 1224 AD
12.0.0.0.0	Tue, Sep 18, 1618 AD
13.0.0.0.0	Fri, Dec 21, 2012 AD
14.0.0.0.0	Mon, Mar 26, 2407 AD
15.0.0.0.0	Thu, Jun 28, 2801 AD
16.0.0.0.0	Sun, Oct 1, 3195 AD
17.0.0.0.0	Wed, Jan 3, 3590 AD
18.0.0.0.0	Sat, Apr 7, 3984 AD
19.0.0.0.0	Tue, Jul 11, 4378 AD
1.0.0.0.0.0	Fri, Oct 13, 4772 AD

The Tzolkin

The "Tzolkin," also called the Sacred Almanac or Sacred Round, is a sacred cyclical count calender which consists of 260 days ("k'in") within the ancient Maya system. It is considered by most to be the region's oldest calendar count. The "Tzolkin" was used to mark the dates for the ceremonies performed on the astronomical new year. In these ceremonies, the priests indicated the days when agricultural plantings and religious ceremonies were to take place within the 260 day cycle. Besides the religious purposes, the calendar was very important for farmers to know when to plant their crops.

The ancient Maya name for this 'divine' 260 day period is not known. The word, 'Tzolkin,' meaning "Division of Days," is a modern word used in the Yucatec Mayan language. The K'iche' Maya call this calendar the "Ch'olk'ij" which means the "Count of Days." The K'iche' and Kaqchikel Maya of modern Guatemala, whom have spoken their variation of the Mayan language for over 500 years, call this calendar: the 'Aj Ilabal Q'ij,' meaning 'Sense of the Day' and 'Chol Q'ij,' meaning the 'Organization of Time.'

It's speculated that the 260 day cycle calender was created to help keep track of the period of time a human baby is carried in the womb from conception to birth, or perhaps the growing cycle of maize from plating to harvest, or even more likely, recording the interval between the solar zeniths which happen at local noon on two different days of the year in the Maya area.

The 'Tzolkin' uses the numbers 13 and 20 are considered to be of great significance to the Maya, as well as all other Mesoamerican cultures. When these two numbers are multiplied together the result is equal to 260, which is the number of days in the Tzolkin calendar before it restarts its cycle.

The Tzolkin calender has twenty days, each with their own names, cycled in a total of thirteen periods known as "trecena." These named days are similar to our modern calendar system's seven named days in the period we call a Week, i.e. Sunday, Monday, Tuesday, etc..

Imix'	Ik'	Ak'b'al	K'an	Chikchan	Kimi	Manik'	Lamat	Muluk	Ok
1	2	3	4	5	6	7	8	9	10
Chuwen	Eb'	B'en	Ix	Men	K'ib'	Kab'an	Etz'nab'	Kawak	Ajaw
11	12	13	14	15	16	17	18	19	20

The 20 days in the Tzolkin with their associated deity glyph (Day Sign) in the modern Yucatec Mayan language.[17]

Each of the twenty days in the Tzolkin are considered to be sacred and are connected to its own deity. So each specific day in a 'trecena' is believed by the Maya to have the personality and characteristics of the deity the day is associated with.

The Maya also use the Tzolkin for the practice of divination in seeking answers to the future. They also used this calendar to know when to perform sacred rituals and religious ceremonies.

The Tzolkin is different than other Maya calendars. For example, the Long Count calender was began on the day believed to be the creation of the human world and then celestial measurements were used to set its length and cycles. In contrast, the Tzolkin's with its 260 day cycle was based from mathematics and wasn't calculated using any natural phenomenon at all. The Tzolkin calendar's spiritual meanings behind its days and cycles were added for the performance of the Maya society's most sacred rituals, celebrations, and religious prophecies.

Usage of the Tzolkin cycle can still be seen being used by the Quiche Maya priests and daykeepers in the Guatemalan highlands. It is also used today by some of the Maya inhabitants in the Mexican state of Oaxaca.

The Haab'

The next calendar the Maya used was called the Haab'. The Haab' is a secular calendar that has no religious or spiritual basis counting a solar year of 365 days. This calendar does not account for the extra quarter-day each year it takes the Earth to revolve around the sun. Our modern calendar corrects for this calculation offset by adding an extra day to February every four years, making a 'Leap Year.'

The Maya didn't calculate for the orbital offset on their Haab' calendar so the dating of their seasons would drift a bit as the years passed. The Haab' calendar was used by the Maya to plan out their agricultural year by planting and harvesting seasons. It was a calendar used to keep track of trade and other day to day record keeping purposes.

All three of the Maya calendars, the Long Count, the Tzolkin, and the Haab' are used simultaneously in Maya dating. The Tzolkin and the Haab' mark and identify the names of the days and Long Count calendar marks, identifies, and counts the years.

The Maya usually marked the date by specifying its location using both the Tzolkin and the Haab' calendars, such as 4 Ahau, 8 Kumku." The Tzolkin date and then the Haab date.

Every Haab' year counts its 365 days, while the Tzolkin calendar's 260 days are counted along with it. One used spiritually for religious ceremonies and rituals and one used secularly for day to day life in agriculture and trade.

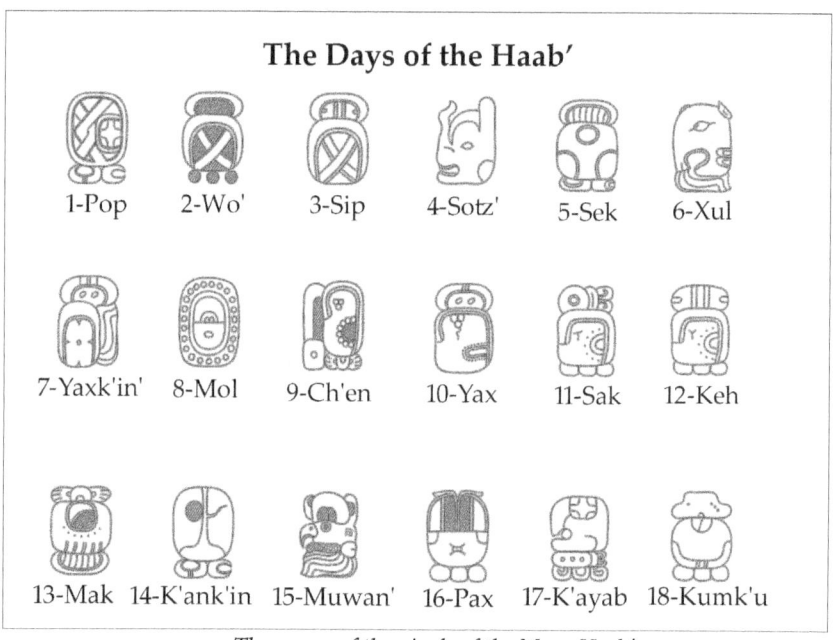

The names of the uinals of the Maya Haab'.

The Haab's 365 day year was divided into eighteen 20-day 'months' the Maya called uinals. These eighteen twenty day uinals made for 360 days of the Haab's year, a completed circle. This left the Haab's year short five days. At the end of each year, the Maya had a five day period of rest at the end of each year called, the "Wayeb."

The Maya believed this was the period of time when the gods rested after a long year. It was during this time, people couldn't count on any support or attention from the gods. During this five day period of the Wayeb, the Maya would perform ceremonies in preparation for the god's return after their rest.

The Wayeb'

The five unnamed days at the end of the Haab' calendar are called the "Wayeb'," This was believed to be a very dangerous time to the Maya. It was believed that during the five day period of the Wayeb', the passageways between the mortal realm and the realm of the underworld opened up. This left no boundaries that prevented the ill-intending spirits and deities from creating havoc and causing disasters to happen. During this time, the Maya had customs they followed and practiced certain rituals to ward off the evil spirits during the days of the Wayeb'.

The Wayeb' glyph.

Some examples of the customs that many Maya followed during the period of the Wayeb' would be practices like trying to avoid leaving their house for the full five days if they could.[281] Bishop Landa wrote that the Maya believed that the time during the Wayeb was considered to be such an unlucky period of time that they didn't wash, comb their hair or do any hard work during these five days. It was treated as a sort of Sabbath where they rested and avoided doing anything. The Maya also believed that anyone born during these days would have a life of bad luck and would remain poor and unhappy for the whole of their lives.[138]

Chapter 12

Ancient Maya Arithmetic

The ancient Maya used a mathematical system that is "vigesimal." A vigesimal counting system is based on 20 units (0 - 19), instead of the 10 unit (0 - 9) based counting system that we use today called the decimal system.

The decimal mathematical system widely used today is believed to have possibly originated by counting the number of fingers that the average person has. Counting with our fingers gives us our ten unit based metric system. It is believed that the Maya possibly began counting with both their fingers and toes, which gave them their twenty based 'vigesimal' system. Their counting system is based on groups of twenty, instead of our modern ten.

When we count using our decimal system, we count to ten and then we add one value to the next tier, or level with a value of ten (10, 20, 30, etc.) for each cycle we reach on tier one (0-9). Using the decimal system, the count of 11 is the value of '1 unit' from "tier 2" and '1 unit' from "tier 1," making the total value equal to 11 (10 + 1 = 11).

Each tier in the decimal system counts up in multiples of ten. 1 x10=100 x10=1,000 x10=10,000 and so on.

tier 3 =	100,	200,	300,	400,	500,	600,	700,	800,	900
tier 2 =	10,	20,	30,	40,	50,	60,	70,	80,	90
tier 1 =	1,	2,	3,	4,	5,	6,	7,	8,	9

Decimal tiers. 1 value from tier 2 is 10 and 1 value from tier 1 is 1, One value each from tier 1 and 2 equals 11 (10 + 1 = 11).

Although we users of the modern decimal system are not used to thinking of our counting in tiers or levels, it does help us understand how the count using the Maya vigesimal system. Just as the decimal system goes by tiers of ten: 1, 10, 100, 1000, 10000, etc., the Maya vigesimal system goes by tiers of twenty: 1, 20, 400, 8000, 160000, etc..

tier	decimal	vigesimal
6 -	100,000	3,200,000
5 -	10,000	160,000
4 -	1,000	8,000
3 -	100	400
2 -	10	20
1 -	1	1

Comparison of decimal and vigesimal tiers.

The modern decimal system has ten possible digits for each placeholder in a tier, numbering from 0 to 9. In the Maya vigesimal system, the first tier's placeholders has twenty possible digits, numbering from 0 to 19.

> decimal tier 1
> 0 1 2 3 4 5 6 7 8 9
>
> vigesimal tier 1
> 0 1 2 3 4 5 6 7 8 9 10 11 12 13 14 15 16 17 18 19

Linear comparison of first decimal and vigesimal tiers.

When the last number of a tier is reached, the count in each system proceeds up to the next tier. Adding a value of 10 in the decimal system or 20 in Maya vigesimal system.

> decimal tier 2
> 10 20 30 40 50 90
>
> vigesimal tier 2
> 20 40 60 80 100 380

Linear comparison of second decimal and vigesimal tiers.

For the number "21," both systems used the twenty from tier 2 and the one from tier 1 to make: 20 + 1 = 21. Except with the Maya vigesimal system, they used 1 value on tier 1 and 1 value on tier 2. The decimal system uses 1 value on tier 1 and 2 values on tier2.

To make "11," the decimal system uses 1 value from tier 2 equaling 10 and 1 value from tier 1. (10 + 1 = 11). The difference in the Maya vigesimal system that value of 11 is actually calculated with two 'fives' from tier 1 and an 'one' also from tier 1. On their system, if the count hasn't reached or passed the value of 20, it remains on the first tier. Additionally, the value of 20 was divided by 4 values of 5.

To represent these values, the Maya came up with two symbols of which they use, a dot and a bar. The Maya used a system of bars and dots for their numbers, instead of representing them by different symbols as it is done in our numbering system. A system the we adapted from Latin and Arabic. Each 'dot' in the Maya system represents the value of 1 unit on a given tier. Each bar represents the value of 5 dots of the tier below it.

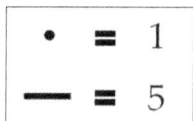

1 dot equals 1 value and 1 bar equals 5 dots.

So when counting to the value of 11, the Maya counted two bars and one dot from tier one (5 + 5 + 1 = 11).

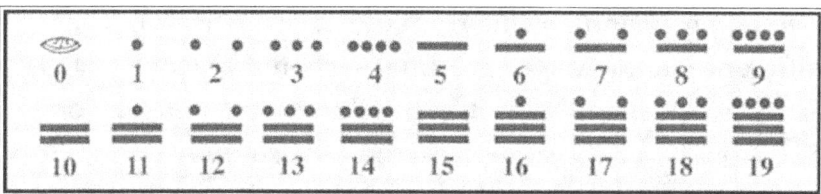

Two bars and one dot on tier 1 equals eleven. The dots go about the bars,

The Maya used a either a cocoa seed pod or a shell to represent the value of 0. They used a system of stacked bars and dots to represent the first 20 numbers.

Table showing first 20 Maya numbers and their Arabic equivalents.[193]

It is believed that because the cacao bean was commonly used as currency throughout Mesoamerica, the Maya symbolized it with a dot to represent one bean. Another reason to believe that the Maya got the idea of using a dot from the cacao bean, is the fact that they packaged their cacao beans in quantities of 8000 to a bag.[255]

The sum of 8000 is one of the place values on the Maya vigesimal system (20^3). The Maya name for the value of 8000 is called a "pic." This is also the name for the sack they used to pack cacao beans in. It's understanding why the Maya found it convenient to call value of 8000 a "pic" and the sack they used that head 8000 cacao beans. A set standard among the Maya for an amount in trade.

The Maya represented written values in a vertical manner, whereas our modern representations of number values are expressed horizontally. For example, we write the number 27 horizontally with the number two then the number seven to the right of it. As the numeric value increases, the number representations are added to the left, continuing horizontally.

The Maya, however, would write the value representation of 27 vertically. Their symbol for seven (a line representing five units with two dots over it) would be on the bottom and the symbol for 20 (a dot on the line above) would be directly over it. The same applies for other numbers. The Maya script or sculptor would fashion their own style of glyph, but the marked value would still be written from bottom to top.

0	1	2	3	4
𝒪	•	••	•••	••••
5	6	7	8	9
—	• —	•• —	••• —	•••• —
10	11	12	13	14
=	• =	•• =	••• =	•••• =
15	16	17	18	19
≡	• ≡	•• ≡	••• ≡	•••• ≡
20	21	22	23	24
• 𝒪	• •	• ••	• •••	• ••••
25	26	27	28	29
• —	• • —	• •• —	• ••• —	• •••• —

Maya horizontal positional value representations.

Maya positional counting displayed values of 20 or more by placing a value symbol over another value symbol. When writing with the Maya vertical vigesimal positioning system, the value of 20 is written with a shell representing zero placed at the base on the bottom position and a single dot, which represents the value of twenty is placed over it in the second vertical position.

A single dot in this position over a zero means one unit of the second tier equaling 20. To write 21, the zero on the first tier would be changed to a single dot (1 unit) and for the subsequent numbers up to 19, counting up to 39.

As they reach the count of 39 again another dot is added to the second position. Any number higher than 19 units in the second position is written using units of the third position.

A unit of the third position is worth 400 (20 x 20), so to write 401 a dot goes in the first position, a zero in the second and a dot in the third. Positions higher than the third are also multiplied by twenties from the previous ones.

Mathematical count

| 20 | 21 | 41 | 61 | 122 | 400 | 401 | 8000 |

Examples of Maya horizontal positional value representations.

The Maya only made one exception to this mathematical order of tiers and that was with their calender calculations. For example, the Haab' calendar's third position only has a value of 360 instead of 400. This is because the calendar only calculates 18 values of 20, or more accurately, the eighteen 20-day uinals (months) of the Haab' year of 360 days (K'in).

Calendric count

| 20 | 21 | 41 | 61 | 122 | 360 | 361 | 7200 |

Examples of Maya horizontal calendric value representations.

165

The Maya names for their numbers are as following:

0 - xix im   10 - lahun
1 – hun   11 - buluc   20 - hun kal   400 - hun bak
2 - caa   12 – lahca   40 - ca kal   800 - ca bak
3 - ox   13 - oxlahun   60 - ox kal   1200 - ox bak
4 - can   14 - canlahun   80 - can kal   1600 - can bak
5 - hoo   15 - hoolahun   100 - hoo kal   2000 - hoo bak
6 - uac   16 - uaclahun   120 - uac kal   8,000 - pic
7 - uuc   17 – uuclahun   140 - uuc kal   160,000 - calab
8 – uaxac   18 – uaxaclahun   200 - ka hoo kal   3,200,000 - kinchil
9 – bolon   19 – bolonlahun   300 - ox hoo kal   64,000,000 – alau

Each set counted by twenties.

21 = hun-tukal = 1 + 20
22 = ca-tukal = 2 + 20
23 = ox-tukal = 3 + 20
24 = can-tukal = 4 + 20
25 = ho-cakal = 5 to 2 x 20
26 = ua-ctukal = 6 + 20
27 = uuc-tukal = 7 + 20
28 = uaxac-tukal = 8 + 20
29 = bolon-tukal = 9 + 20
30 = lahun-cakal = 10 to 2 x 20
31 = buluc-tukal = 11 + 20
32 = lah-ca-tukal = 12 + 20
33 = ox-lahun-tukal = 13 + 20
34 = can-lahun-tukal = 14 + 20
35 = ho-lahun-cakal = 15 to 2x20
36 = uac-lahun-tukal = 16 + 20
37 = uuc-lahun-tukal = 17 + 20
38 = uaxac-lahun-tukal = 18 + 20
39 = bolon-lahun-tukal = 19 + 20

Numbers held great significance in the Maya culture. For example, the number 20 signifies the total number of digits a person has: 10 fingers and 10 toes, or five digits on four limbs. As all five digits on a single limb is $1/4^{th}$ the value of a whole of 20, or the value of tier 1.

The number 13 refers to the number of major joints in the human body where the Maya believed disease and illness entered the body. These joint locations were: one neck, two shoulders, two elbows, two wrists, two hips, two knees and two ankles for a total of thirteen.[252]

It's these two numbers, 20 and 13, that are used to make up the Tzolk'in calendar. The Tzolk'in is believed to be the first calendar used by the Mayas. The number 13 is also the number of levels in heaven where the Maya believed the Sacred Lords ruled the Earth.

The Value of Zero

The ancient Maya had discovered and used zero. They usually represented the value of zero or null with the symbol of an ovular shell. The Long Count calendar requires the use of a zero as a place holder within its vigesimal numerical system. There have been many different glyphs that were used as a zero symbol by different scribes for marking Long Count dates.

Glyph writing was a respected form of art to the Maya. At Chiapa de Corzo, Mexico, the earliest known use of glyphs being used as zero was discovered on 'Stela 2' located there which dates to 36 BC.

The concept of zero is attributed to first being understood and utilized by the Hindus. The Hindus were also the first to use the concept of zero in the way it is used today. A symbol was required in positional numbers to mark the place of a power at the base of a value that was not actually occurring. To mark no value in a value position. This was indicated by the Hindu by a small circle called a "Shunya." This is the Sanskrit word for 'vacant.'

By the middle of the second millennium BC, in the ancient civilization of Babylon the lack of a positional value for zero was indicated by a space between their symbols of numerals.

The Babylonians used a sexagesimal counting system that had the value of 60 at its base. This was the same sexagesimal system that was also used by the ancient Sumerians during the third millennium BC. They had passed down their system of mathematics to the ancient Babylonians.

In 498 AD, the Indian (Hindu) mathematician and astronomer Aryabhatta introduced the decimal system when he stated, "Sthanam sthanam dasha gunam." This statement means, "place to place in ten times in value." This may have been the origin of the modern ten-based decimal value system used today.

The ten number based system used with the Hindu decimal zero was adopted by Arabian mathematicians. They had further modified it and introduced the decimal system and the concept of zero to the Europeans during the Middle Ages.

There are two concepts of zero. One concept is that as being a placeholder in the numbering system to indicate the absence of numbers in a numbering column. This usage was known by the ancient Babylonians and surprisingly, also by the Maya some centuries before. The zero representation used by the Maya civilization didn't look like ours and was used slightly differently because their number systems stacked and wasn't ten-based system.

The other concept of zero is that as being a "null number', or what you get when you subtract 1 from 1. Instead of being a placeholder for the absence of a value, it is the value of nothing. This concept was not developed until some time later. It is estimated to have been realized by at least after 600 AD, but nobody knows exactly who had came up with this concept, or exactly when.

It is speculated that it could have been the Arabic mathematicians, but there is no documentation to be that certain.[151]

Since the eight earliest Long Count dated artifacts appear outside of the main Maya homeland, it is assumed that the use of zero in the Americas pre-dates the Maya civilization and was possibly the invention of the Olmecs. Many of the earliest Long Count dates were found located within the center areas of the Olmec civilization which had already ended by the 4th century BC. These Olmec artifact dates are several centuries before the earliest known Long Count dated artifact that has yet been found.

In addition to understanding the concept of 'zero,' there are some examples in the Mayan language that tell us that the Maya also understood the notion of infinity.

Here are some examples:

- *"Hun tso'dz'ceh,"* to count the hairs a deer has.
- *"Maxocbin,"* infinite in number.
- *"Hunhablat,"* countless.
- *"Picdzaac(ab),"* long number, countless.
- *"Ox'lahun D'zakab,"* eternal thing.
- *"Hunac,"* countless times.

The Maya used a vigesimal numerical system that's based on sets of 20. In a true twenty based system, the first number denotes the number of units up to the value of 19. The next set would denote the number of 20's up to 19 times until the sum value is 400. The next set of numbers are the 400's up to 19 times and so forth up to the next set.

This rule of the vigesimal is followed by the Maya with the exception of when it was used for calenders in the third place value only the numbered of to the 360's, instead of the number of the 400's. This is because of the 18 20-day uinals that make the 360 days in the Haab' year.

This vigesimal mathematical system is used in the writing used by the scribes that wrote the Dresden Codex. It's the only math system of the ancient Maya for which we have any written evidence of. This is the number system used by the Maya priests and astronomers for celestial and calendaric calculations.[253]

Besides calendars and dating, the Maya needed a counting system they could easily use on a day to day basis. A counting system that would have been used by merchants and traders. This had to be a commonly known numbering system that was used in daily speech when communicating amounts.

The Maya commonly used a dot to represent one value using a cocoa bean or a pebble for counting. We can speculate that they may have perhaps used a stick as a horizontal bar to represent 5 and other special symbols to represent the values of 20, 400, or 8000, an amount of which we know they called a 'pic'.

Although no trace of such a counting method remains, we can reasonably speculate that the Maya used a simple numbering type counting system of such as pebbles and sticks. The count could be higher with this method with higher numbers being calculated by repeating or removing the sticks and pebbles as many times as was needed to make the count.[253]

The Maya vigesimal 20 based counting system has been found in use through numerous different archaeological discoveries. The Maya used mathematics for a wide spectrum of things. However, it should be noted that it is extrapolated by some that the Maya did not have methods of multiplication for their numbers and definitely did not use division of numbers. This cannot be true as the Maya counting system is certainly capable of being used for the operations of multiplication and division.[253]

The Maya vigesimal system still tends to confuse people. Counting that goes 1, 20, 400, 8000, 160000, etc., can seem complicated and confusing when you're trying to figure out how it was useful to anyone except to very 'bright' Maya?

As mentioned earlier, the decimal system is based on ten which we can get by counting our fingers, 1 - 10. Whereas, the Maya counted all the way to twenty by counting all their fingers AND toes to 20. We use the decimal system and count in sets of 10, the Maya used the vigesimal system and counted sets of 20. Each set of 20, goes up the next level and is then counted in sets of 20 again and so forth up each tier or level.

That can get rather confusing when you're not used to counting like that. What about a way to count simple things in "Maya 20 count way" without being very good at it?

The Four Slave Example

In the "Four Slave" example, we make the assumption that the ancient-era individual counting is using the fingers and toes of four slaves they have in possession to count out a 'pic' of cacao beans. A "pic" in Mayan is 8000. The ancient Maya packed cacao beans in sacks of 8000, which is a pic. Thus, we assume it takes four Maya slaves to count and pack a 'pic' of cacao beans, without actually knowing how to count. Here is how we do it:

To count 8000 cacao beans with 4 slaves that cannot count, all you need to do is make sure they have all their fingers and toes.

- Take "slave 1" and have them pick a cacao bean for each finger and toe they have (20). When they have a cacao bean for each finger and toe, they put that sum into a single pile of cacao beans. They then pass their pile of cacao beans to the next slave, "slave 2."

- "Slave 2" then keeps a stack of cacao beans they get from "Slave 1" for each finger and toe that they have. Once they have a stack of cacao beans from "Slave 1" for each finger and toe they have, they combine it into one stack. They then pass their stacks to the next slave, "Slave 3," whom cannot count either but also has all their fingers and toes.

- "Slave 3's" job is to watch what the other slaves are doing and when "Slave 2" has enough stacks for each finger and toe they have, "Slave 3" gets passed "Slave 2's" stack. "Slave 3," whom proudly caught on easily, then makes a stack for each finger and toe they have from the stacks "Slave 2" passes them.

- "Slave 4" has the easiest job, all he has to do is wait until "Slave 3" has enough stacks from "Slave 2" for each finger and toe. Once "Slave 4" gets passed "Slave 3's" pile, "Slave 4" only has to put the stack of cocoa beans he gets from "Slave 3" and put them in a sack and let his master know, "they have a 'pic' of cacao beans."

None of the of them may be able to count past 20, much less to 8000, but they can still accurately pack 8000 cacao beans - as long as all the slaves have all their fingers and toes.

When you look at it in this perspective, Maya arithmetic isn't so difficult and you can see how it can be simplified and used in everyday trade. In addition to the significance that they understood the concept of 'zero' before Europeans did, which opened the door for advanced mathematics and science.

Personally, I was pretty satisfied with the "Four Slave" example. It made sense in a primitive society, making that ever regretful assumption that they were all thinking in very basic forms. We tend to underestimate human curiosity and when we do that, we' make false assumptions and forget that the Maya had complex planetary calculations that we've just been able to calculate and verify with the assistance of modern computers. The Maya didn't have computers, powerful telescopes, or any the modern equipment and teams of scientists that we have in the modern age. Or did they?

Well, as wonderful a fantasy as it may be, I am pretty certain aliens from another world or dimension didn't visit and teach the Maya the mathematics necessary to calculate the universe's celestial bodies. It is also safe to assume, aliens probably did not arrive in flying saucers and build the temples and structures of the ancient Maya civilization.

The Maya certainly needed a higher understanding of mathematics beyond basic cacao bean counting to accurately calculate the paths of celestial bodies, timing and patterns. You need higher math for the engineering necessary to build the structures that they built, many that stand to this day. After all, you can only go so far with lucky block stacking.

With this in mind, we need to consider a simpler system to count and perform basic arithmetic. Just in case we don't have any slaves or our slaves are missing some fingers and toes.

The Grid System

If you don't have any slaves left over from the last raid on the neighboring city, you could always use the grid system to count and do your arithmetic. The "Grid System" is basically what it sounds like. You use a system of grids to do your addition and subtraction.

The grid system works extremely well in the Maya stacked vigesimal system. This is also a wonderful exercise tool that can be used to teach Maya numbers, adding and subtraction, and help to better to better understand the Maya counting system in general.

You start by making a simple grid. You can make a grid the ground using sidewalk chalk or by using masking tape on a table. Gather up some stones and small sticks. Or you can use items that you may have around, such as beans and Popsicle sticks, for example. Begin by making two grid squares, side by side. Start the count by placing one bean in each grid square.

Examples of how the Grid System works in simple Addition:

A single bean or 'dot' in each square is how the value of "1" is measured and conveniently, also written in Maya. The value of one is a single dot.

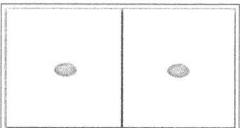

For simple addition, we have a single bean or dot in each square representing 1 + 1.

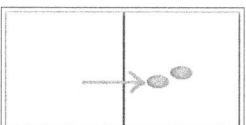

We add our 1 + 1 by sliding the beans from the left grid (grid A) into the grid on the right (grid B), making our total count equal to 2 (1 + 1 + 2).

We'll try another example by adding 3 + 3. We take three beans, representing the Maya symbol for the count of 3 in each of the two grid squares.

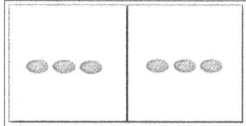

Here, we have 3 in grid A and 3 in grid B to add.

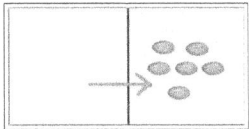

We take all the beans in grid A and slide them all into grid B to be summed up.

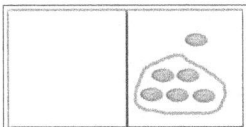

Remember, in Mayan, five dots equals a bar. So we gather 5 beans and we exchange them for a bar, or stick.

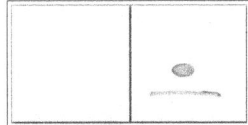

After removing the 5 beans and exchanging them for a stick (bar), we have the represented sum of 6. This is also properly represented in Maya writing, as six is written with one dot over one bar.

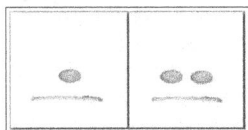

In this example, we will add 6 and 7, represented by 1 bar and 1 dot in grid A and 1 bar and 2 dots in grid B.

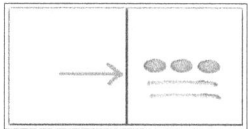

We again, push all the sticks and beans from grid A into grid B. We then add the number of bars (sticks) and dots (beans) to get a total count of 13 (two 5's (bars) + three 1's (dots) = 13).

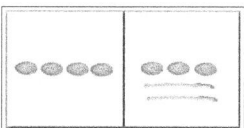

Here, we shall add 4 and 13.

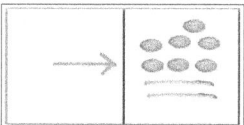

We move all the dots and bars from grid A into grid B.

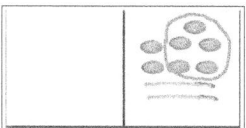

Remember, gather every group of 5 dots and exchange them for 1 bar.

We add the exchanged bar and have our sum of 17.

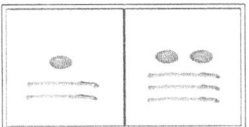

Let us continue by trying to add 11 and 17 together.

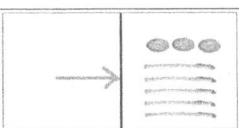

Move all the dots and bars into grid B.

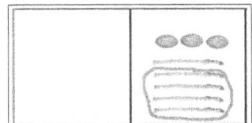

We now remove 4 bars to make 1 dot for the next tier, because four 5's equals 20 and the count moves up a value in tier per 20 values on the previous tier.

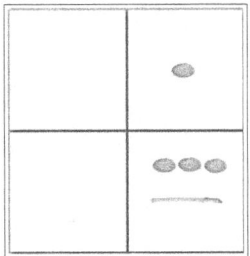

We remove the 4 bars from tier one and exchange it for a single dot in tier two representing the value of 20. We add a single dot in the 20 tier plus 3 dots and a bar in the ones tier and our sum is 28 in total (20 + 5 + 3 = 28).

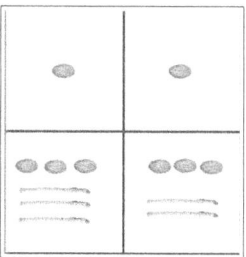

Here we begin our addition using two tiers (the 1's tier and the 20's tier). On tier two, in both grids, we have a dot in place of the 20. On tier one, we have our sums 18 and 13, making the total as 38 + 33.

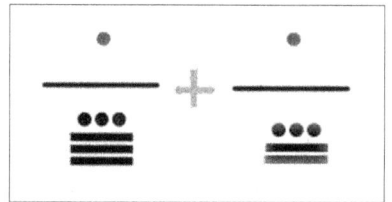

Example of 38 + 33 written in Maya.

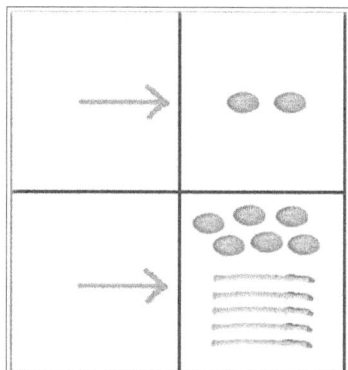

Again, we move all the beans and bars from grid A into grid B, staying in the tier levels of each grid.

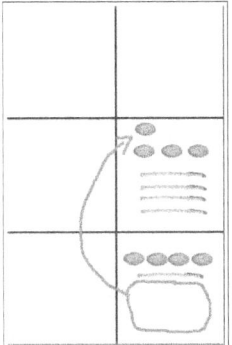

Starting on the bottom tier, we remove each group of 4 bars and exchange them for a bean to place in the second tier group.

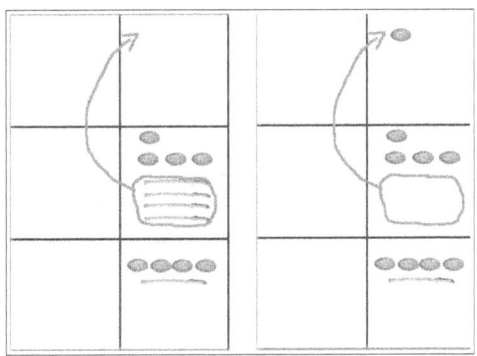

Next, on tier two, we again remove any groups of 4 bars and exchange them for a dot for the next level tier up, tier 3 (20^2).

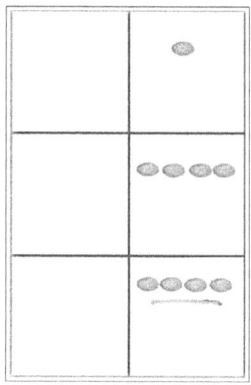

And now we have, as it would also look if written in proper Maya, the sum of 489.

$(400 + 1) + (20 + 4) + (4 + 5) = 489.$

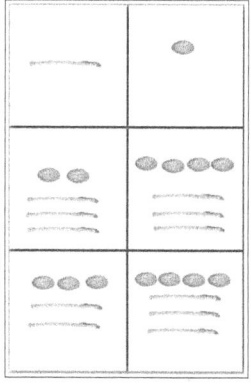

Let us try another on three tiers.

We shall add 2373 + 799, without counting past 5 to get our total.

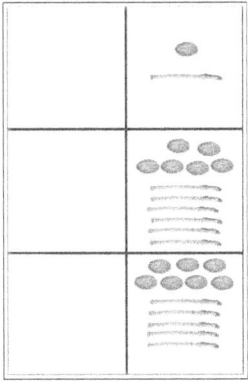

As before, we move all the dots and bars from grid A and slide them all into grid B, staying in whichever tier level they were in.

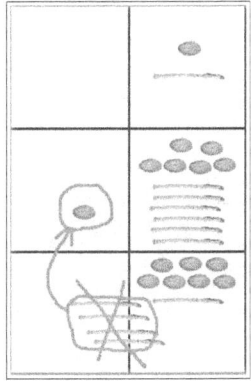

We begin by starting on the bottom tier and add groups of 4 bars and exchange them for a dot to the next tier level up.

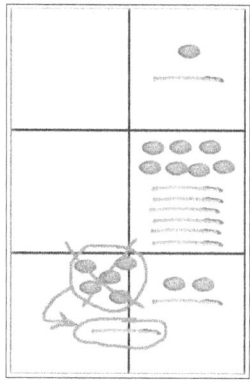

We also exchange all the groups of 5 dots for bars, if you hadn't already done so.

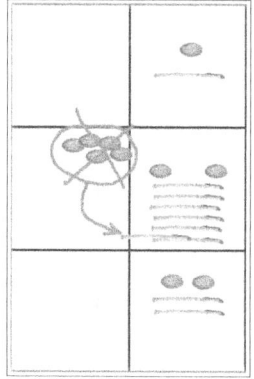

We continue by going up the next level tier and add a bar for every 5 dots.

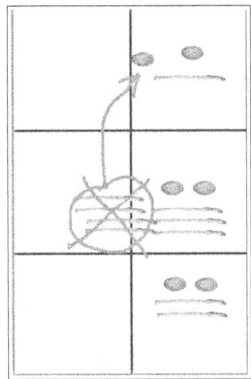

We also add a dot to the next level tier for every 4 bars that we have.

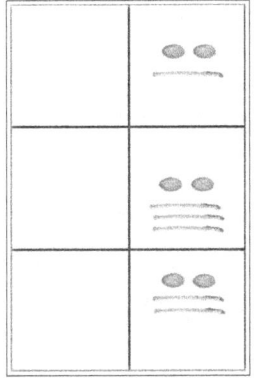

And now we have the sum of 3152.

Subtraction

The grid system works with subtraction as well as it works with addition. The except is when we subtract in Maya, we borrow from 20, instead of 10 like in the decimal system.

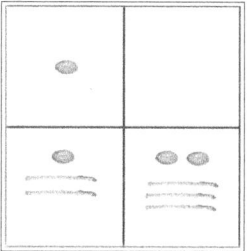

In this example, we shall subtract 17 from 31 (31 – 17).

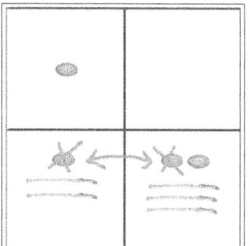

Subtract first the lowest value, in this case the ones. Remove one dot in grid B for one dot in grid A. To Subtract, you remove a value from one grid and match and remove the same value in the other grid.

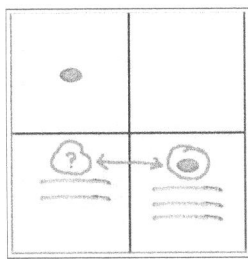

At this point, we've run out of dots from grid A. To resolve this, we remove 1 bar in exchange for 5 dots in grid A.

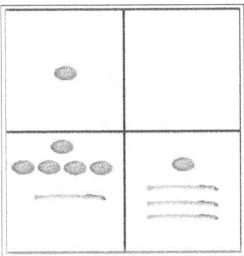

Here, we're exchanged 1 bar in grid A for 5 dots.

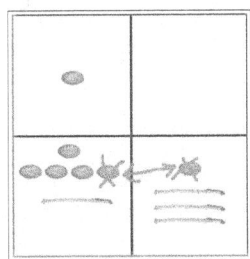

We then continue removing dots in grid A for every dot we have left in grid B.

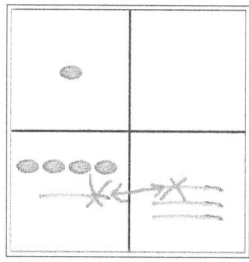

And continue subtracting by removing every bar from grid A for every bar in grid B.

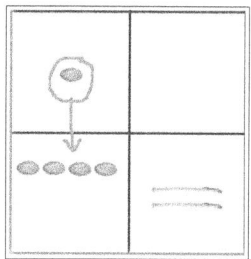

Now that we've removed every bar in grid A for every bar in grid B, we find that we are short bars in grid A because we still have 2 bars in grid B to subtract. In this case, we borrow from tier two and subtract 1 dot (value = 20^1) and add 4 bars to tier one in it's place.

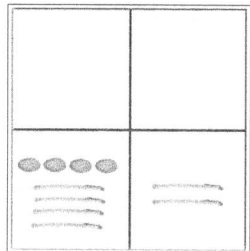

By borrowing from tier two, we now have bars in grid A to remove for the remaining 2 bars we have left in grid B.

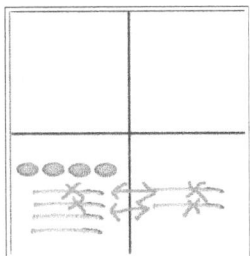

Continue subtracting bars in grid A for every bar grid B has.

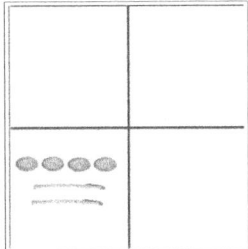

Now that we've removed every dot and bar from grid A that we had in grid B, we finish with our total of 14.

$$31 - 17 = 14$$

The Finger Method

Simple calculations can also be made using the Maya vertical vigesimal system without grids, beans, or bars. If we were conducting trade or simply needed to do some simple and quick math. Gathering slaves to help count using their fingers and toes is not very convenient and what if we were a lower status merchant or priest and didn't have any slaves to help us count.

Making a quick "grid system" on the ground would work, but we'd still have to gather sticks and stones to do the counting and that's no good in a hurry.

So we must reason that the Maya would have simplified their system of basic counting so they could count on their fingers, like we do with our decimal system of 10s. Simply using all our fingers and toes to count to 20 is NOT convenient, especially if you had your shoes on. The Maya simply had to have an easier way to count through their base system of 20 with just their hands.

The Maya didn't count linear in 20's like our current modern system does with 10's. Additionally, the Maya didn't have specific characters to designate specific numbers, like the Arabic system that uses specific symbols for 0, 1, 2, 3, 4, 5, 6, 7, 8, 9. They used a system of dashes (lines) and dots to represent a value. A tiered stack of lines and dots to represent the sum of a number, not actually having a specific symbol to represent the number.

In fact, the Maya method of writing numbers never counts past four dots or three bars. The symbols always changes and goes up to the next value. A count past 4 dots is exchanged for a bar (value=5) and 4 bars (4x5) is a dot on the next tier valued at 20. This is how they could have huge, long count numbers with relatively few symbols to represent the amount. The Maya didn't count using all ten fingers to reach the count of 10, they only used two fingers to represent 10.

Assuming the Maya counted in the same manner as we do, counting each finger with a value of 1. They would stop with using four fingers and then would use a seperate finger to represent the value of 5. WJereas, when we use our fingers to count, we use all five fingers on our hand to display the vlaue of 5. The Maya only needed to use their fingers to count up to four dots, then count a bar and then bars with dots and so forth. The value of 6 was one bar and one dot, or one finger from each hand, representing a bar and a dot.

To count using the Maya vigesimal system, on one hand each of your four fingers represents a value of 1. On the other hand, each one of your fingers represents a value of 5. When you count, you count on your hand with the value of 1 in sequence of 1, 2, 3, 4. then drop those and add a value of 1 on the other hand.

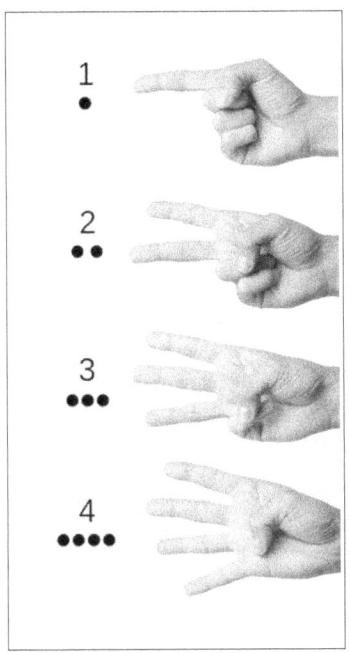

On the first hand, count: 1, 2, 3, 4.

When you reach 5, close the fingers on the first hand and you raise 1 finger on the other in the value of 5.

One finger on the other hand represents five fingers on the first hand.

On the first hand, you continue the count: 6, 7, 8, 9.

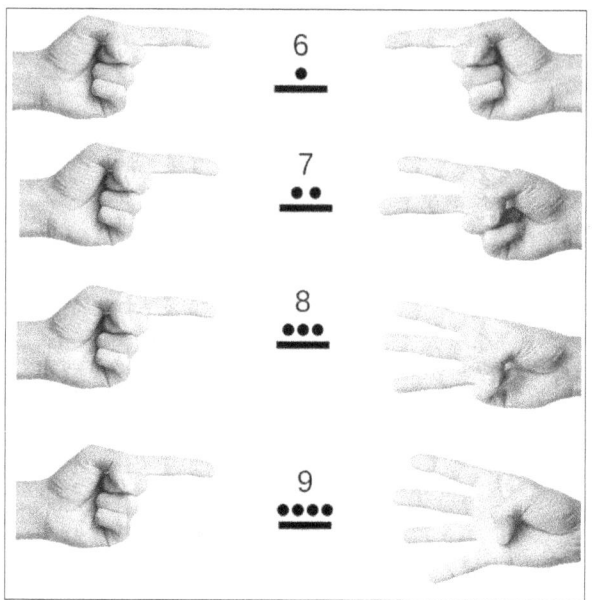

Each finger on the left hand = 5, and each finger on the right hand = 1.

When you reach 10, all the fingers on the first hand go down and the second hand now displays two fingers representing the value of 10 (5 + 5).

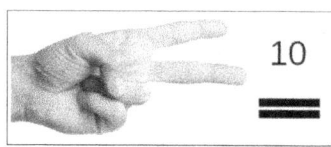

The value of 10 is represented by two fingers on the second hand (5 + 5 = 10).

On the first hand, with two fingers on the second hand out, you continue the count: 11,12,13,14.

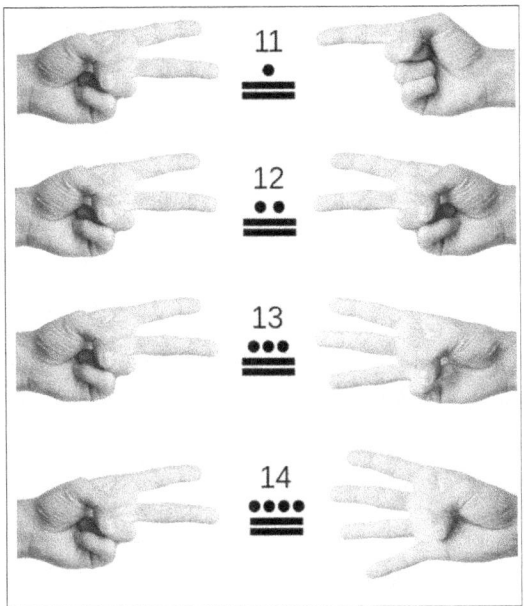

Then at the count of 15, raise an additional finger, totaling to three fingers which represents the value of 15 (5 + 5 + 5).

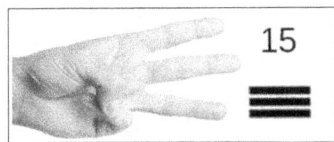

Thus, with three fingers out on the second hand, we continue the count on the first hand with: 16,17,18,19.

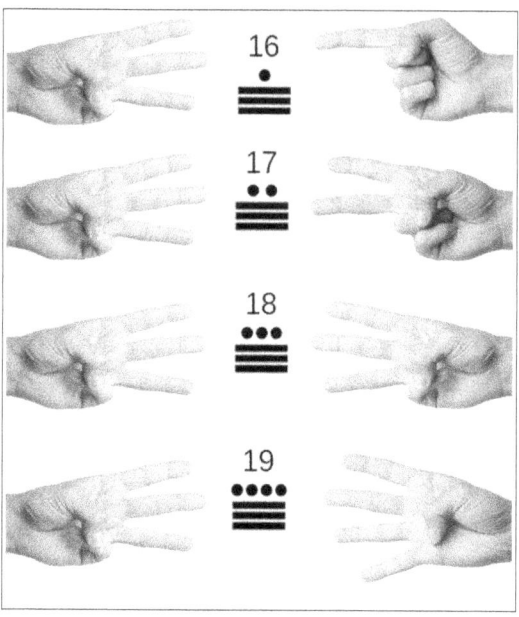

At the count of 20, you close the fingers on the first hand and display all four fingers (or alternatively use your thumb) on the second hand to the value of 20 (5 + 5 + 5 + 5 (or with the thumb representing 1 value on the second tier, which equals 20)).

Wow, that is amazing, I think we just unlocked the mystery to a Maya simplified counting system. We can easily count to 20 with just our two hands and use the same dot and dash system to represent counts of 1 for dots and dashes as 5s.

The count is not in linear values counting to 20, it is in the value of ones and fives and their relative position of counting up in segments of 4 and 5, with the sum of 4 or 5 being the next value, represented by the next symbol and position. Simply, when four of the the "fives" are used up in their sequence, they go to the next level or tier.

The value of one and five also changes as it goes up each level. This is why there are no number symbols in Maya counting, only dots for values of 1 and bars that represent the value of 5 dots. There is no "20," there is only one dot on a tier, which merely represents the value of four bars on the previous, lower tier.

Using the 'finger method,' you can even alter the system slightly and give each thumb the value of 20 (one dot each on tier two in Maya thinking). With both thumbs having the value of 20 each, equaling 40 (2 x 20). The value of 'one' for each finger on the first hand (4 x 1), and the four fingers on the other hand with each valued at 5 (4 x 5). We can easily count to 64 (20 x 2 + 4 x 1 + 4 x 5) with just two hands. Whereas, previously we could only count to 10 using the same fingers with the decimal system.

Interesting as well, that we can count to 64 with our hands using the Maya system. It appears to be a number significant to a computer's binary method of counting using on and off switches that we call bytes. There are 8 bits to a byte. A row of 8 bytes is 64 bits. Of course this multiplies up to 128, 256, 512, etc., which I am sure you recognize as numbers used in computers as: gigabytes (GB), megabytes (MB) and Kilobytes (KB).

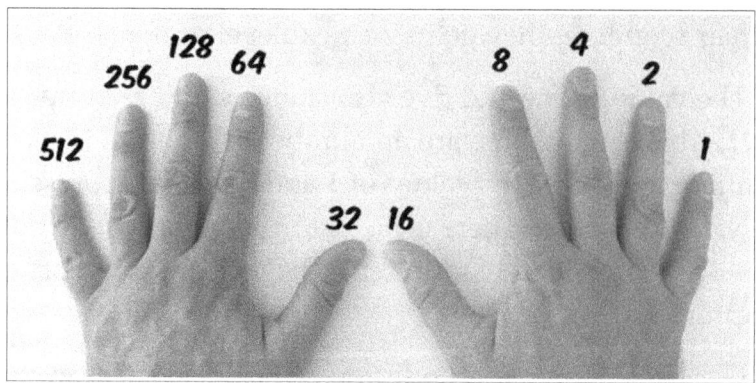

Number values for using fingers to count in Binary System.

A computer or calculator counts using a binary system of off and on switches, each with a value of 0 or 1. This is broken down into a sequence of 1, 2, 4, 8, 16, 32, 64, 128, 256, 512 typically.

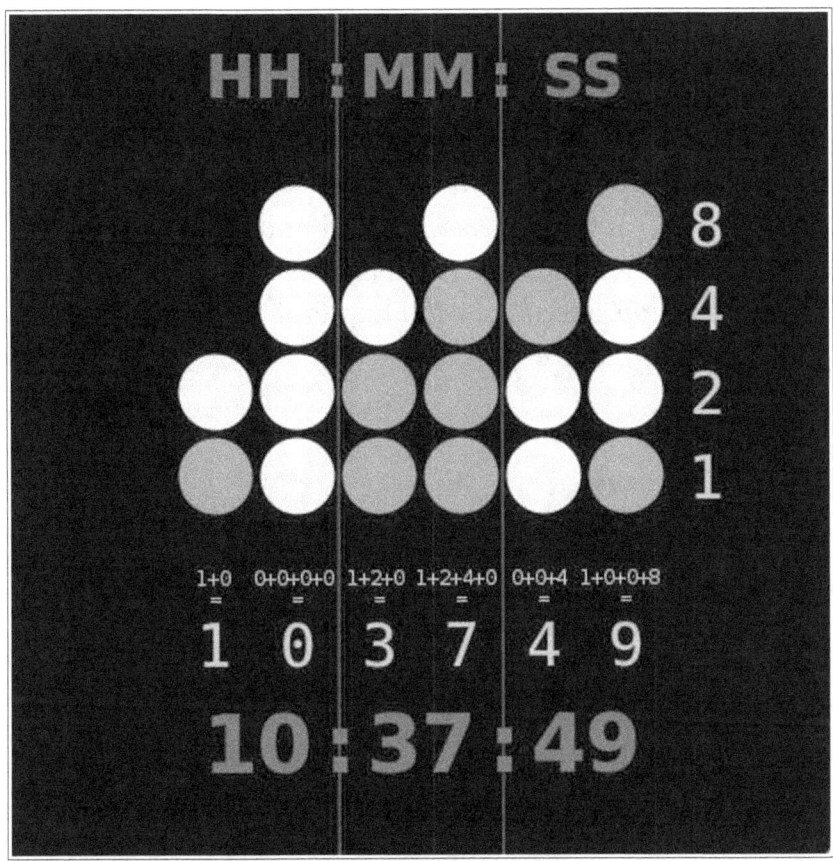

Visual explanation of a binary clock..[256]

A binary clock might use LEDs to express binary values. In this clock, each column of LEDs shows a binary-coded decimal numeral of the traditional sexagesimal time.

Without going into greater detail about binary counting and how to calculate using the binary system, we can see how the Maya counting system is similar to the binary system computers use. This means the Maya could use their system to perform complex calculations needed to accurately plot astronomy, calendars, and the mathematics necessary for the engineering feats they had achieved.

The Maya system of counting with your fingers is great, but you do eventually run out of fingers and toes and would like an improved way to do basic arithmetic. This where we take it to the next level and build an abacus (plural abaci or abacuses). An abacus is also called a 'counting frame' and is a calculating tool that is used for performing arithmetic processes.

The Maya Abacus

The Mesoamerican abacus is called a "Nepohualtzintzin."[257] The arrangement of the Maya Abacus, or Nepohualtzintzin, is with seven beads or balls (or cacao beans) per level. Every level higher unit sum is equal to the sum of all the units of one level less than it. the first level being twenty units of one. alue the sum of level up in the Maya counting system, represented in illustration 1 by white lines, labeled: A, B, C, D, E, and F.

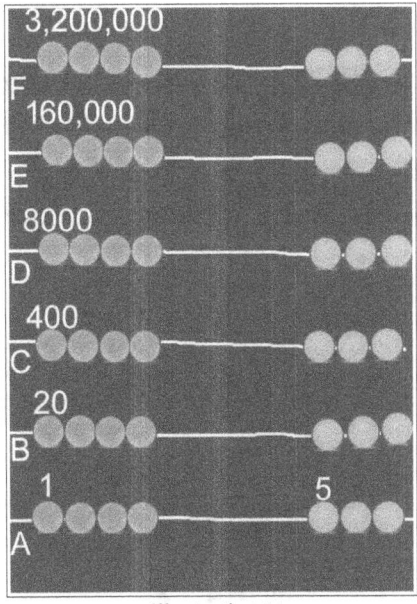

illustration 1

The represented value of the beads on each level in these examples are:

Blue beads = 1 unit.

Red beads = 5 units.

Each level's unit increases in value each level up, as represented by white lines in *illustration 1*, as follows:

Line A = 1,

Line B = 20,

Line C = 400,

D = 8000, E = 160000, etc.. as shown in *illustration 1*.

Using the Nepohualtzintzin is much like using any other the World's various abacuses through time. You begin the count on the first line, line A (level or tier 1), by sliding a blue bead to the middle of line, counting to 1 (see *illustration 2*).

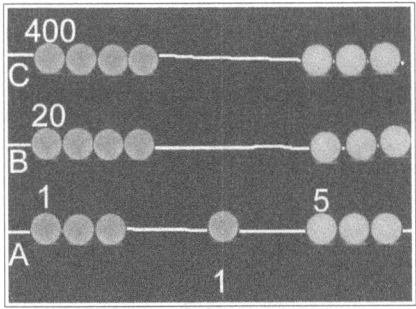
illustration 2

The absence of any beads in the middle of any line would be zero and represented with a shell in written Mayan. Continue counting up with your Maya Abacus by adding blue beads.

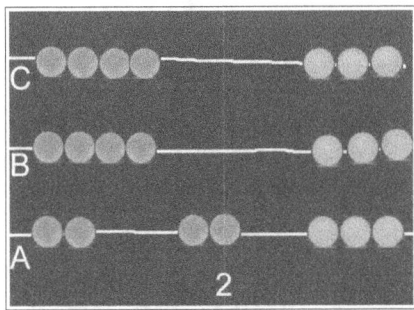
Illustration 3

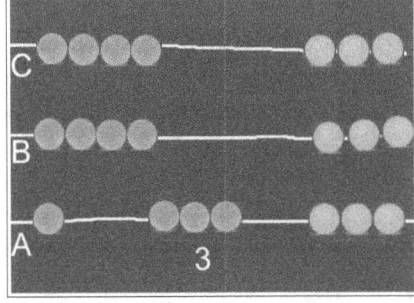
Illustration 4

When you've used all four blue beads counting to 4,

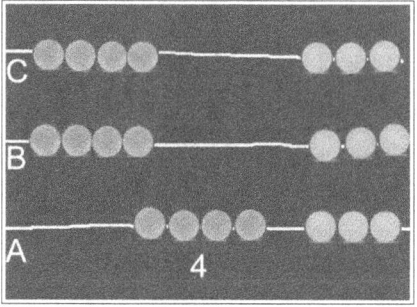

Illustration 5

Slide all the blue beads back to their original position and slide one red bead, value 5, to the middle to make the count at 5. as displayed in *illustration 6*.

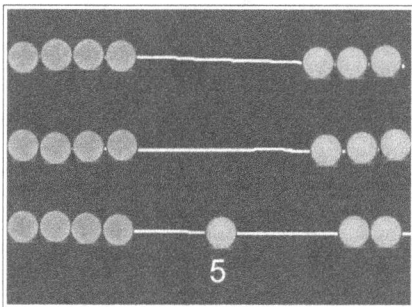

Illustration 6

The count continues by adding a blue bead next to the red bead, making the sum 6.

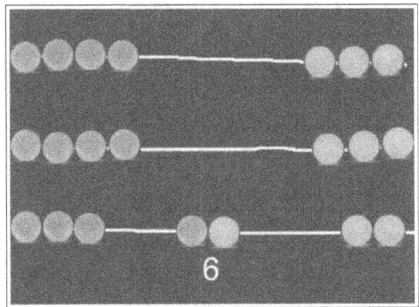

Illustration 7

Continue adding on line A with blue beads, counting up 7, 8, and 9. Ten is then counted by returning the blue beads to their original position and sliding an additional red bead (value is 1 red unit = 5 blue units) to the middle (5 + 5 = 10).

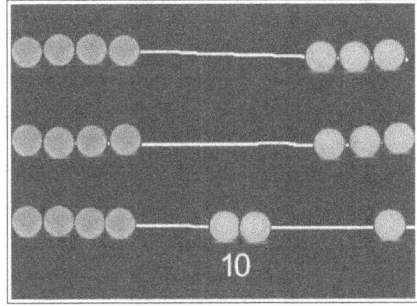

Illustration 8

An additional red, adds 5 to the count, making the sum 15.

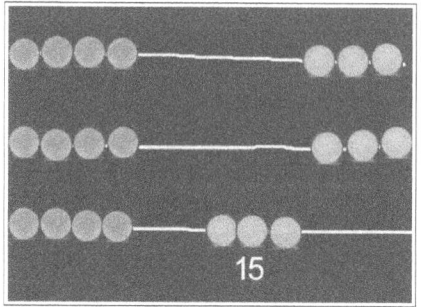

Illustration 9

The count continues by adding blue beads, counting up 16, 17, 18, and then with all red and blue balls in center equals 19. (*illustration 10*).

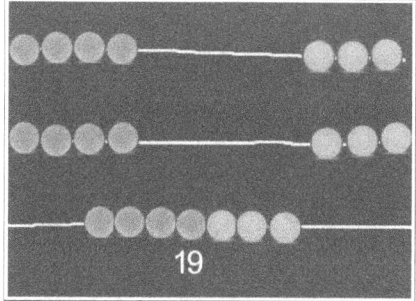

Illustration 10.

Continue counting up to 20 by sliding all the beads on line A back to their original start positions and slide 1 blue bead on line B (valued at 20 per unit) to the middle.

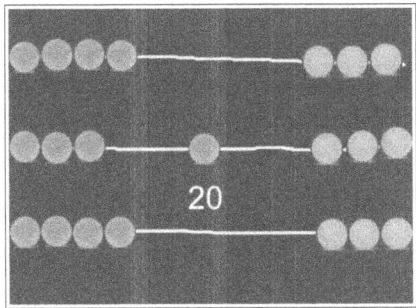

Illustration 11

A single blue bead in the middle of the second level (line B) brings the count to 20. When writing this number, you would add a shell on the bottom tier to represent zero as a place holder.

Increase the count by adding 1 blue bead on the first line, line A (illustration 12).

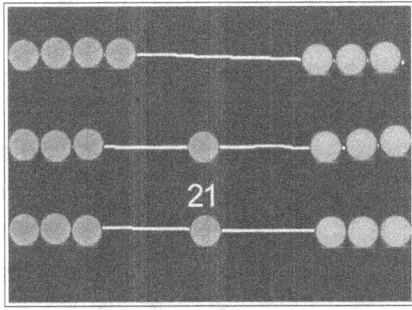

Illustration 12

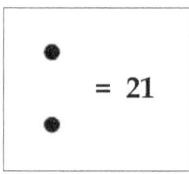

Some additional examples of using the Maya Abacus count:

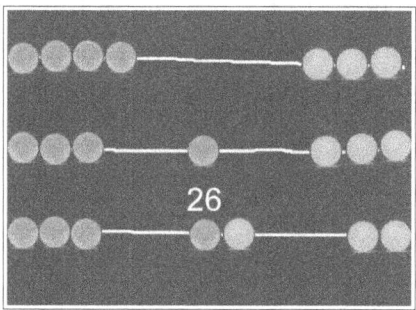
Illustration 13

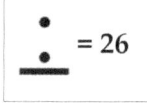

Remember, each blue bead is the value of 1 unit and each red bead is the value of 5 single units, with the value of each unit starting at 1 on the first level and increased 20 times the value of a single unit value of the line (1, 20, 400, 8000, etc.).

In *illustration 14*, one red bead (value = 5) on line two, representing 5 blue beads (value 1 unit = 20), shows the total of 100.

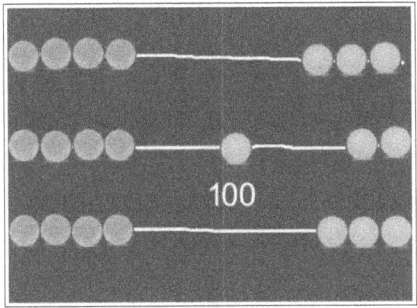

Illustration 14.

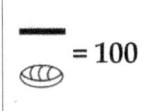

We then increase the count to 111 by adding two red beads on line A, valued at 5 units each and 1 blue bead on Line A, valued at 1 unit (100 + 11 = 111).

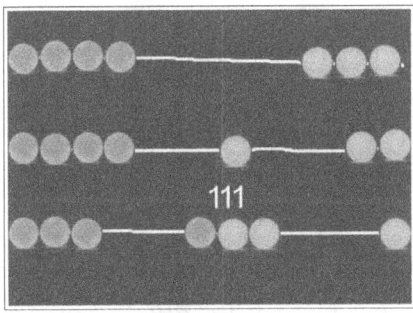

Illustration 15.

We set the count at 400 by adding 1 blue bead on line C (3rd level). We know that the value of the single blue unit bead on the third level are worth 400 because the sum of a units on the 3rd level are equal to the sum of all the units from the previous level, which were valued at 20 per unit, which is the sum of all the units on the 1st line which are valued at 1.

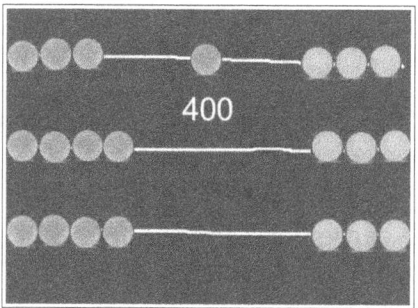

Illustration 16.

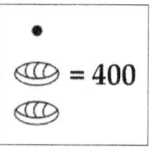

When we write 400 in Mayan, we write a single dot on the 3rd level and a single shell on each level under it, on the 1st and 2nd levels, as seen under *illustration 16* above.

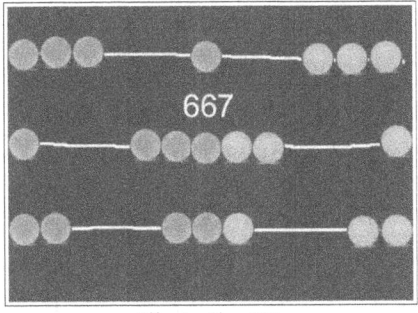

Illustration 17.

(1 x 400) *Line C*

+

(13 x 20) *Line B*

+

(7 x 1) *Line A*

= 667

The development of the Nepohualtzintzin, or Mesoamerican abacus explains the magnitude of understanding that the Mesoamericans had in mathematics.

Knowledge in these mathematics made it possible that they were able to make such exact calculations of universal cosmogony. The Nepohualtzintzin, which essentially was a pre-Hispanic computer, was not only able to make mathematical calculations, but also astronomical and gestation interpretations. The Nepohualtzintzin as an instrument that is similar to other abacus in different cultures, such as the Japanese soroban.

The abacus helps make it possible to perform not only basic operations such as: addition, subtraction, multiplication and division, but it also can be used for complex operations like roots, powers and integral and differential calculus operations.

The word "Nepohualtzintzin" comes from the Nahuatl language and is formed by the roots; Ne - personal -; pohual or pohualli - the account -; and tzintzin - small similar elements. This roughly translates into: counting with small similar elements by somebody.

The knowledge of the Nepohualtzintzin and its use was passed on to students, whom dedicated their entire lives from childhood to mastering and calculating the events and movements of the skies.

Unfortunately, the Nepohualtzintzin and its teachings were among the victims of the evangelizing paranoia of the Spanish Conquest. The Nepohualtzintzin proves that Mesoamercian cultures already had great capabilities in scientific and technological developments prior to the arrival of the Europeans.

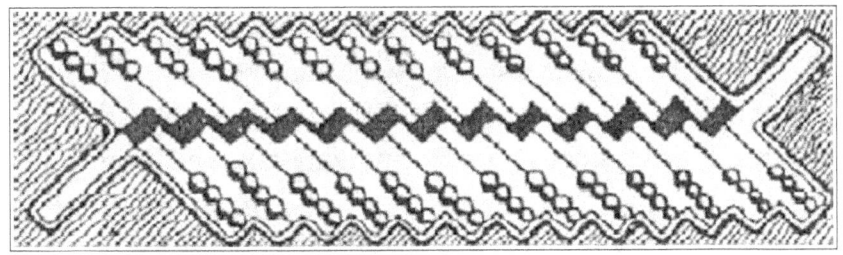
A typical Nepohualtzintzin usually has 13 rows with 7 beads in each row.

A Nepohualtzintzin has 13 rows with 7 beads in each row, which makes for a total 91 beads.

- The 91 beads in the Nepohualtzintzin represent the number of days in a season within the year.
- Two Nepohualtzitzin make a total of 182 beads, which is the number of days of corn's cycle from sowing to harvest.
- Three Nepohualtzintzin making for a total of 273 beads and is the number in days of a human baby's gestation time from conception to birth.
- Four Nepohualtzintzin complete the cycle of a year's time, minus a day and a quarter.

The Nepohualtzintzin accounts for the absolute precision needed for the higher scientific and mathematical levels that the Mesoamericans had developed many years before the arrival of the Spanish conquistadors.

David Esparza Hidalgo's had rediscovered the Nepohualtzintzin upon finding diverse engravings and paintings of the ancient Mesoamerican math instrument in Mexico. Very old Nepohualtzintzin that were discovered could have also been attributed to the Olmec culture. Some of the ancient abacus that have been found were usually in the shape of bracelets, especially those discovered in the Maya area. One of the ancient Nepoualtzitzin abacus appeared on a painted vase in Guatemala known as the "Nejar Vase."[257]

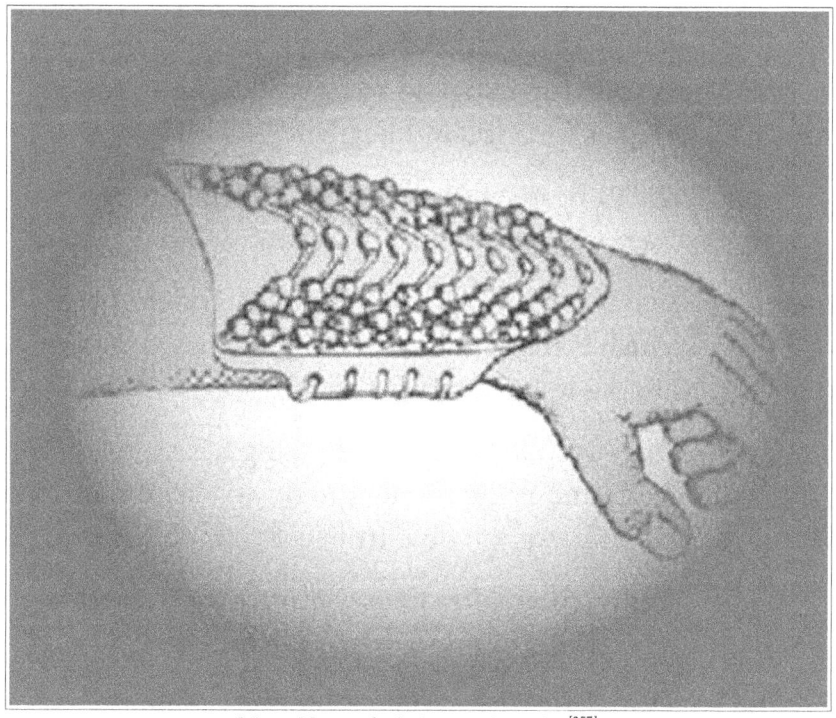

Maya Nepoualtzitzin as a Bracelet.[257]

The existence of the Mesoamerican abacus gives us insight that the ancient Maya already had the sufficient knowledge to devise and handle a device of mathematical complexity and also extend its usage into their daily lives and activities.

Maya concept of Fractions

The word fraction comes from "fractus," the Latin word for broken. It represents a part of a whole or any number of equal parts of the whole. Broken or fractured from the whole.

A common, vulgar, or simple fraction consists of an integer numerator, which is displayed above a line (or before a slash), and a non-zero integer denominator, displayed below (or after) that line. The numerator represents a number of equal parts and the denominator indicates how many of those parts make up a whole. For example, in the fraction ¾, the numerator 3 on top, tells us that the fraction represents 3 equal parts, and the denominator, 4 on the bottom, tells us that 4 parts make up a whole.

In contrast to previous claims by researchers, the Maya were familiar with a notion of fractions or "parts of a whole." To indicate parts in general, they used the term "tzuc" which literally means "part." The Mayan words, "tu," "can," "tzucil," and "ban cah," equals the four parts of the World (cah), or the four quarters of the whole World.

For the notion "¼," we find the expressions, "heb" (to open) and "u" (moon).

Some examples:

- "heb u" = moon opening or open moon.
- "hun heb u" = 1/4 moon or moon opening of ¼.
- "ca heb u" = 2/4 moon or moon opening of ½.
- "ox heb u" = 3/4 moon or moon opening of ¾.

For the notion of "½," two possible applications can be found.

First, in distance:

- "Tan coch" = half, in the middle.
- "lub" = "legua" (5.5 km).
- "tan coch lub" = half a "legua."
- "tan coch tu cappel lub" = in the middle of the second legua (5.5 km), or 1 ½ "legua."

Secondly, in time divisions, such as:

- "tan coch kin tu cappel" = in the middle of the second day = 1 ½ days.

"Xel" = dividing the unit in two and subtracting one part. Xel is in fact a negative fraction:

- "xel u ca kin bé" = - ½ + 2 days = 1 1/2 days;
- "xel u ca cuch" = - ½ + 2 loads = 1 1/2 loads;
- "xel u cappel lub" = - ½ + 2 leguas = 1 1/2 legua;
- "xel u yox katun" = - ½ + 3 katun = 2 1/2 katun;
- "xel u ca kal" = - ½ x 20 + 2x20 = -10 + 40 = 30;
- "xel y yox bak" = - ½ x 400 (bak) + 3 x 400 = 1300.[143]

From these astronomical and time keeping divisional uses in the Mayan language, the best inference we can gather as the most common use of fractions would be quarters or fifths of a whole that reflects the use of the Maya counting system in it's self.

Typically, a bar being a whole and thus is divided into five equal parts, as five dots equals one bar. So, we're able to assume the Maya also had a regular use of 5ths (1/5, 2/5, 3/5, 4/5, and 5/5 = 1 whole).

However, a better inference would be to conclude that fractional systems were in the Maya vigesimal system, no different that regular counting. That in fact, the entirety of the Maya vigesimal system is already fractional.

There are two kinds of scientists;

1. Those who can extrapolate from incomplete data

So, how is it possible to write and use fractions in the Maya system? On the second tier, the single dot (value = 20) would be the whole number (or denominator). On the first level below it (count 0 - 19), would be the fractions (numerators) of the upper whole.

In this example, is the Maya count for 20 (20^1). We then express this whole number as a fraction using Latin numerals.

$$\frac{\bullet}{\text{shell}} = \frac{20}{20}$$

We could extrapolate by saying a good way to indicate a Maya fraction would be to use the shell (used for the null or zero placeholder) as the placeholder for an incomplete whole when written as a fraction. We use a shell on top to represent an incomplete whole of the dot, whereas when we use a shell below the dot on the bottom tier to represent a whole count of 20 on the second tier. To represent the fraction, we remove the dot on the second tier and replace it with a shell and the shell is now a placeholder indicating an incomplete whole number.

For example, the fraction 1/20th could be expressed in Maya as:

Using the shell (0) as a placeholder for the dot of the whole of 20. The bottom number, the numerator, is the fraction amount of the whole (20^1).

$$\frac{🐚}{\bullet} = \frac{1}{20}$$

$$\frac{🐚}{—} = \frac{5}{20} = \frac{1}{4} \text{ (or 0.25 or 25\%)}$$

$$\frac{🐚}{=} = \frac{10}{20} = \frac{1}{2} \text{ (or 0.5 or 50\%)}$$

$$\frac{🐚}{\equiv} = \frac{15}{20} = \frac{3}{4} \text{ (or 0.75 or 75\%)}$$

Addition of fractions is carried out the same manner as regular addition by simply adding the sums together.

$$\frac{16}{20} + \frac{12}{20} = 1\frac{8}{20}$$

Chapter 13

The Maya Codices

The Pre-Columbian Maya scribes and priests created and kept whole libraries of books that recorded information about their history, beliefs, astronomy, and calendars. Unfortunately, most of these books were systematically destroyed during the Spanish Conquest. Almost all the books of the Maya were burned because the Christian conquistadors believed they containing writings about the devil.

There are three of these books, called Codices, that have managed to survive today. There are other codices known to be in existence, but there are the only three Maya codices whose authenticity are not questionable.

These three Maya codices are:

•**The Madrid Codex**, or the "Tro-Cortesianus Codex."

•**The Dresden Codex,** or the "Codex Dresdensis."

•**The Paris Codex**, or the "Peresianus Codex."

Pre-Columbian Maya books are called 'codices'. These codices are folded manuscripts made with long strips of paper that are folded in a zig-zag pattern like a screen. The Maya made the paper from the inner bark of some of the various species of local fig tree (*Ficus cotonifolia or Ficus padifolia*). To make this paper, they harvested the inner bark of these trees and then pounded it into pulp with stone implements called "bark beaters."

The pulp was mixed with natural gums, which worked as a bonding substance that held the paper together. A thin coating of fine white lime was then applied on both sides of the sheets of paper, much like gesso, to create a smooth finish on the surface. The scribes would then paint their hieroglyphs on this surface, telling the stories of historic or religious events.

They also wrote about celestial events and recorded the significant happenings of important figures.

Scribes painted on both sides of the paper when they created these codices. They were read by reading from left to right along one side of a paper strip. The codex strip was then turned over and reading continued on the other side.

The Tibetans often wrote their books in this very same manner. Whereas, flipping over the entire page in order to read the other side as we would turn a page to the other side to read the next page. During this same time period, Europeans write on scrolls, rolling the text.

The Paris Codex

The Paris Codex was rediscovered in the year 1859 by León de Rosny in the Bibliothèque Nationale (National Library) in Paris. The Codex had been forgotten over the years. When de Rosny rediscovered the codex, it was tucked away in a basket of old papers that were in a chimney corner. The Codex was wrapped in a piece of paper that had the name, "Pérez" written on it.

The codex used to be called the "Codex Pérez," or sometimes "Peresianus," because of the name 'Pérez' that was written on the paper that was wrapped around it when it was 're-discovered.'

It has also been called the Codex Mexicanus, because of it being discovered in Mexcio.

It is now formally known as the **Paris Codex** to prevent any other confusion with another 19th century compilation of early Colonial Maya writings that is also called the Codex Pérez.

Only a segment of the complete Paris Codex exists today. There are only a total of 22 of the original screen-folded pages of the codex that have managed to survive.

The pages of the codex measure 12.5 cm horizontally and 23.5 cm vertically. Some of the fine white lime coating has eroded from the edges of the pages, this has caused some of the hieroglyphs and images to become lost.

The scribes painted the pages of the codex in many colors, using black, red, turquoise, yellowish-brown, blue, and pink. The outlines of the hieroglyphs and images were painted in black.

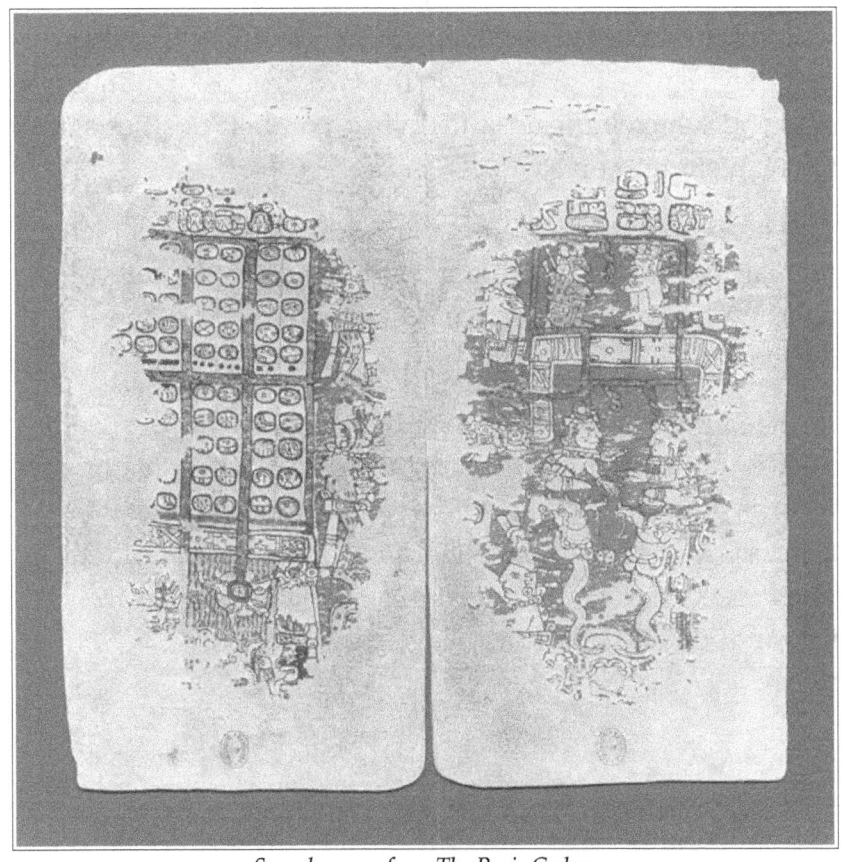

Sample pages from The Paris Codex.

In these pages of the Paris Codex is a rendition of the spirit world. At the top of leaf 22 are the four seated "Bacab," Hobnil, Cantzicnal, Saccimi, and Hosanek, which are associated with the four cardinal world directions. They are responsible for holding the sky up, the seasons, and the four winds. They are akin to the Norse's "Four Dwarves," Norðri, Suðri, Austri and Vestri. whom also hold up the sky at the four cardinal points and control the winds.

Below the Four Bacab on the leaf are two death deities, which can be partly identified by the "death-eyes" collars that they're wearing. Between the two groups of deities is a skyband which indicates the division of their positions in the heavens and on earth.

These two realms were separate, but the scibe depicted them as being tied together as part of a unified whole by painting green skyropes that twist and weave among the figures.[107]

The Paris Codex was a record book Maya scribes made that contained information on calendrical cycles, historical records, the gods and spirits, weather patterns, and astronomy. Of the four surviving codices, three verified, The Paris Codex is unique because it includes historical information and describes Maya constellations.[105][106]

The Madrid Codex

The Madrid Codex is also known as the Tro-Cortesianus Codex. It is one of the three surviving pre-Columbian era Maya books that dates back to the Postclassic Period in Mesoamerican history, from around 900 to 1521 AD.[101] The Madrid Codex is held in the Museum of the Americas (Museo de América) in Madrid and is considered to be the most important piece in the museum's entire collection.

The Codex was made from long strips of amate, a Mesoamerican paper made from the inner bark. The pages were folded up accordion-style like a screen. This paper was also coated with a thin layer of fine stucco. This coating was commonly used as the painting surface on most items, similar to applying gesso on a canvas.

The complete Madrid Codex consists of 56 amate sheets that are painted on both sides, making for a total of 112 pages. A portion of the book called, "the Troano" is the larger part of the codex consisting of a total of 70 pages. These are pages 22 through 56 and pages 78 through 112.

The Troano portion of the codex takes its name from Juan Tro y Ortolano, whom was the original owner of the pages brought from the New World.

The other 42 pages that make the Madrid Codex are from was originally called the 'Cortesianus Codex.' The Cortesianus Codex portion make for pages 1 through 21 and pages 57 to 77 in completing the Madrid Codex. Each amate page in the Madrid Codex is roughly 23.2cm by 12.2cm, which is 9.1 inches long by 4.8 inches wide.[102]

The writing in the Codex is stylistically uniform on the pages which suggests that the book was the work of a single scribe. However, upon closer inspection of the different glyphic elements shows that there were other scribes were involved in the book's writing. The Codex is perhaps the work of as many as eight or nine scribes whom wrote different parts of the manuscript.

The religious content of the codex makes it likely that the scribes were somehow related to the Maya clergy or even priests themselves. It is also more in likely that the codex was passed down from scribe to scribe and each scribe that received the book added a section to it in their own unique style. Further adding to the knowledge within the book.

The content within the Madrid Codex are mostly records and knowledge to be passed on. It contained mostly different celestial and calender almanacs that were used to help plan the timing of ceremonies and when to perform divinatory rituals. There aren't as many astronomical tables in the Madrid Codex as there are in the Paris Codex and the Dresden Codex, but the tables are present. Some of the content is most likely to have been copied from older Maya books written by scribes past.[103]

Scenes in the Madrid Codex connected to the hunt.[104]

The images in the Madrid Codex also depict rituals such as human sacrifice and ways of invoking rainfall. There are also writings of everyday activities such as beekeeping and about hunting. There are depictions that range from warfare to weaving. These careful ink paintings give us a close glimpse into Maya day to day life.

The Dresden Codex

The Dresden Codex is a Post-Classic era Maya book written in the eleventh or twelfth century by the Yucatecan Maya people located in Chichén Itzá, half a millennium before the arrival of the Spanish.[95] This Maya codex, also called the Codex Dresdensisis, is believed to be a copy made by a scribe of a much older original text that was probably written 300 to 400 years earlier during the Late Preclassic Period of Maya history.[96]

The Dresden Codex is perhaps the oldest book written in the New World. Historians believe it to be the oldest book from the Americas in existence. All other copies had been destroyed by fire when the Spanish had conquered the region.[97]

The Dresden Codex consists of thirty-nine sheets with writing on both sides, making for 78 pages. The overall length of the Codex laid completely out is 3.56 meters, or 11.7 feet long. Originally, the manuscript had been folded in accordion style folds like the other Maya Codices. But, today it is spread out in two parts and exhibited at the Museum of the Saxon State Library located in Dresden, Germany.

The Dresden Codex is exhibited in two halves, each of them are approximately 1.8 meters, or 5.9 feet in length. There are four pages in the Codex which are empty, as it may have been a work in progress. Each two-page sheet in the book measures 20.5 centimeters (8.1 inches) by 10.0 centimeters (3.9 inches).

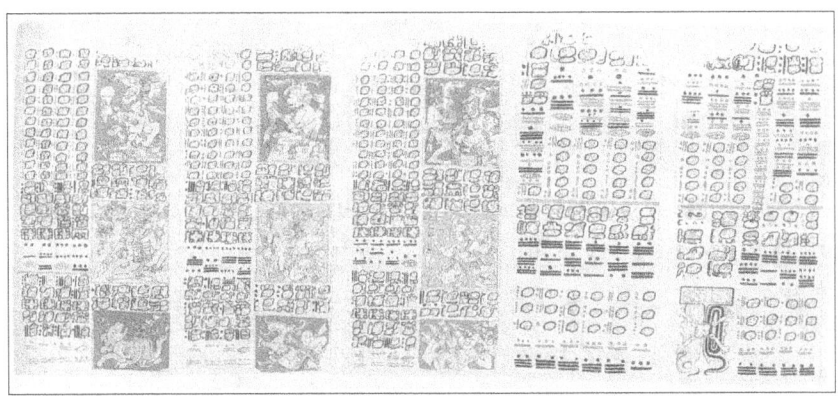

The Dresden Codex, pages 47, 48, 50, 51, and 52.[98]

Johann Christian Götze, whom was the Director at the Royal Library at Dresden, Germany, had purchased the codex in Vienna from a private owner selling it in the year 1739. The identity of who the private owner was or how it came into their hands and in the Austrian city of Vienna is unknown.

It is speculated that the Codex was sent as a gift by the Spanish Conquistador Hernán Cortés to King Charles I of Spain as a tribute in the year 1519. King Charles had appointed Hernán Cortés as the Governor and Captain General of the newly conquered territory in the New World, then known as New Spain.

Like the other codices, the Dresden Codex is made from

a Mesoamerican amate paper sometimes called "kopó." The paper used in these codices were made from the pulp of the fig tree's inner bark that's been flattened out and coated with a lime fine stucco paste used as a 'gesso.' The book is then folded in the same accordion-like, zig-zag form called leporello. Folding books in this same manner was common in how other Mesoamerican culture's texts were written and stored.[99]

The codex was written by six different scribes whom used both sides of the paper sheets when they wrote out their scripts.[100] Each scribe had their own particular and unique writing style and added their own individual style to the glyphs they painted on the surface of the pages.

The glyphs and images painted in the codex were carefully painted by the scribes with extraordinary care using very fine brushes. The basic colors they mostly used were red, black, and Mayan blue. These colors were the most used in the codex. The images were painted with inks that were made of vegetable dyes.

The Codices have been extremely useful in helping decipher the Mayan written language. In the Dresden Codex, of the 350 signs and glyphs approximately 250 of them have been fully deciphered. Most of these glyphs refer to the accompanying figures depicted on the pages. Each glyph full of information and telling it's own story.

Most of the glyph writings inside the pages are short phrased remarks about an image they accompany. There are also numbers used in the codex that consist of using bars for the value of five, dots used for the value of one and shell depictions to represent "zero" or null.

The Dresden Codex also contains the records and many depictions of astronomical tables that are very accuracy to this day. The Codex is mostly famous for the lunar sets and planetary table of Venus that are written within its pages. The Lunar Series has precise intervals marked which even includes to occurrences of eclipses. These cycles are still accurate measurements. The Venus table also accurately measures the sky movements of the planet Venus.

The codex also contains almanacs for farmers with both astronomical and astrological tables. The Codex also kept ritual schedules that went along with the celestial tables. The specific numeral references in the book have to do with the complete 260-day ritual cycle of the Tzolkin calendar.

The Dresden Codex includes many instructions that are suppose to be conducted at certain times of the year, even certain new-year ceremonies to were be performed as well. These are careful descriptions of the Rain God's various locations at certain times of the year in order to perform rituals to summon rain when needed.

Chapter 14

Maya Religion

Religion had already existed for more than two millennia as a recognizably distinct phenomenon within the Maya culture. This religion had spread over to many other indigenous cultures throughout Mesoamerica. Each distinct culture with their own variations in local traditions and practices.

Today there is movement of Maya descendants that seek to reinvent the old traditions by merging them with new traditions. The modern Maya religion of today coexists and interacts with various other belief systems and religions, including those of Christianity and its various denominations.

Traditional Maya religion had become more of a generalized belief system that is often referred to locally as "costumbre," which means 'customary.' The "costumbre" are referred to as the customary local religious practices, in contrast to the established Orthodox Roman Catholic ritual that was brought by the Spanish.

To a large extent, the modern Maya religion is a

complexity of ritual practices from various beliefs that are both new and old. The practitioners of the modern Maya religion in the indigenous Yucatec villages are usually priests who are referred to as "jmen," which means in their language, 'practitioner.'

The core of Maya religious practice, both that of the new combined ways and those of the ancients, is the unfailing performance of ritual

Ritual is among the main concepts which relates to Maya religion.

The Maya landscape is a ritual topography that is rich with many significant landmarks such as mountains, wells and caves, all of which have been assigned to specific ancestors and deities.

The Tzotzil town of Zinacantan is surrounded by seven 'bathing places' which are dedicated to various mountain-dwelling ancestors revered by the Maya. One of these sacred waterholes serves as the residence of the ancestor's nursemaids and laundresses.'[126]

Many important rituals also took place at or around or around many other landmarks in the Yucatán, such as the karstic sinkholes (cenotes). All of these sites were considered sacred to the ancient Maya.

The geographical lay-out of shrines and temples wasn't the only thing that governed ritual locations, some locations were set by the projection of calendrical models onto the landscape. An example of this would be when certain sacred location casts a shadow upon a certain spot at different times of the year.

The Maya also had specific combinations of day-names and numbers which were ascribed to specialized shrines in the mountains and other religious landmarks. The location of the Sun at a certain time of the year or the position of a planet or star relevant to the location of the shrine would also signal when it was the appropriate time for their ritual use.[127]

Another sacred location in the northwestern Maya highlands is where the four days, or 'Day Lords', who start the year are assigned to four mountains. The entire landscape itself was also considered sacred and signaled when and where certain rituals took place during the year.

For example, during the early-colonial period of the Yucatán, the thirteen katun periods and their deities were sectioned onto the very landscape which was conceived as a 'wheel' and were said to be successively 'established' or attached to specific ancient Maya towns.[128]

Many things signal when rituals were to take place, but the biggest source was in their various calendars. The main calendars which governed ritual were: the divinatory cycle of 260 days, which was important for individual rituals, kept on the Tzolkin and the calendar year of eighteen months kept on the Haab', which determined the pace of the public feasts.

There were also very elaborate New Year celebrations that were witnessed being performed on the Yucatec kingdom of Maní that were described by Diego de Landa. [138] It is not known how widely this festival cycle was shared by other Yucatec kingdoms, or if it was also valid for the earlier Maya kingdoms. These were observations were few and not much more was recorded about them.

Our limited Knowledge of Pre-Columbian Maya religious practices and beliefs come from a limited variety of sources. Some of these primary sources are the three surviving and authentic hieroglyphic books, the Maya Codices: The Dresden, The Madrid, and The Paris Codices, all of which date from the Post-Classic period after 900 AD.

Additionally, we get some of our information from what are called the 'ceramic codex' (the corpus of pottery scenes and texts) and from surviving mural paintings on Maya ruins. These are the sources from which we've gained much of our knowledge from from the Classic (200 AD - 900 AD) and Late Preclassic (200 BC - 200 AD) periods of Maya cultural development.

Our knowledge about Maya religion during the Columbian Period comes from sources such as; the Popol Vuh, the Ritual of the Bacabs, and, at least in part, from the various Chilam Balam books.

We also rely on an abundant of our information from gathered journals and records from Spanish treatises made during the Colonial Period. Such records and descriptions as those from Diego de Landa for the Lowland Mayas and Las Casas for the Highland Mayas. These is also lexicons such as the early Motul (Yucatec) and Coto (Kaqchikel) dictionaries that were created.

Offerings and Sacrifices

Sacrificial offerings were a religious activity in Maya culture which involved either the killing of animals or the bloodletting by members of the community in rituals that were superintended by priests. Sacrifice has been a feature of almost all ancient societies of the World at some stage of their development and for broadly all the same reasons: to fulfill a perceived obligation towards their gods.

Archaeological data has continued to expand on this subject as more excavations take place, confirming much of what the early chroniclers had written about it. A major breakthrough was the deciphering of the Mayan syllabary in the 1950s AD. This decipherment allowed the glyphs that were carved into many of the temples to be read and understood.

This was in addition to the lifelong work of Mayanist, David Stuart who was made famous in the film, "Cracking the Maya Code." Excavation and forensic examination of human remains have also thrown light on the age, sex and cause of death of sacrificial victims. The reason for sacrifice was that the Maya believed that the only way for the Sun to rise was for them to sacrifice someone or something everyday to the gods. Their prisoners were mainly attackers from other people.

Animal sacrifice and blood-letting was a common feature in many Maya festivals and rituals. Human sacrifice was far less common, as that sacrifice was tied to bigger events such as: ill fortune, warfare, and the consecration of new leaders or temples. The practice was also far less common than in the later Aztec societies who performed it more regularly in comparison. When human sacrifice did occur, the Maya would sacrifice prisoners, who were most often taken from neighboring kingdoms.

Sacrificial offerings serve to establish and renew relations ('contracts', 'pacts', or 'covenants') with the 'Other World.' The choice, number, preparation, and arrangement of the offered items such as: special maize breads,[129] maize and cacao drinks and honey liqueur, flowers, incense nodules, rubber figures, and even cigars,[130] obey to stringent rules.

Chapter 15

Maya Mythology

Maya mythology refers specifically to the pre-Columbian Maya civilization's extensive and deeply rooted polytheistic and animistic set of religious beliefs. These beliefs had been long established by the time the earliest known distinctively Maya monuments had been built. The inscriptions on these monuments depict their deities and they pre-date past the first millennium BC. A time when much of Europe was coming out of the Stone Age and entering the Bronze Age.

There's considerable diversity in the various Maya religious narratives that have been found. Among the best known myths are those about the opening of the Maize Mountain by the Lightning deities, the struggle of Sun and his Elder Brethren, and the marriage of the Sun and Moon.

The early creation mythologies are found in the Popol Vuh and in some of the books of Chilam Balam. But they are limited in information and are supplemented by writings and depictions on other sources.

One of the most important sources for Classic Maya

mythology are still scenes which are painted on pottery (the so-called 'ceramic codex') fragments that have been found and monumental iconography found on nearly all Maya structures.

The two principal narratives recognized thus far in Maya mythology are about the Hero Twins and the principal maize god. These narratives had to be reconstructed from painted scenes and reliefs in which often the narrative and ritual concerns related were often intertwined in description.

The oldest written myths that have been deciphered date from the 16th century AD. These are found in the historical documents and journals from the Spanish in the Guatemalan Highlands. The most important of these documents is the Popol Vuh, which contains within it the Quichean creation story and some of the trials and adventures of the Hero Twins, "Hunahpu" and "Xbalanque."

The Yucatán is an equally important region and source for Maya myth and legend. The Books of Chilam Balam contain mythological passages of great antiquity. There are also mythological fragments which are found scattered among the early-colonial Spanish chronicles and reports, which were usally written by clergy. The chief amongst them being Diego de Landa's "Relación" and in the dictionaries that were compiled by other early Spanish missionaries.

In the 19th and 20th centuries AD, anthropologists and local folklorists have committed many of these translated stories to paper. Even though most Maya tales are the results of Spanish narrative methods which have intermixed with Mesoamerican traditions. They are a wealth of information because some of the tales translated reach back well into pre-Spanish Colonial era.

In some cases, the ancient Maya myths may only have been preserved by neighboring peoples who told their story. The narrative of the principal Maya maize god and that of the Bacabs are examples of these kinds of preservations of Maya mythology.

As the process of hieroglyphical decipherment continues, captions with explanations begin to be included into the depicted scenes. Eventually the complete story will be restored to their original eloquence and make ancient narratives come back to life more fully so we can understand them better.

We have also learned in translations, that in Maya folk religion, the deities which govern the wild vegetation, the game animals, and fish are considered as being "owners." This concept is much like their reverence to the 'Mountain-Valley' deities (or mountain spirits) of the Guatemala highlands.

From all of these translations, deciphers, and recordings of Maya folk traditions, we're about to put together much of the base of ancient Maya mythological beliefs.

The Legendary Hero Twins.

A degree of veneration through Maya rituals, ceremonies, and religious practice went towards the legendary Maya Hero Twins. The Hero Twins are best known through the 16th century AD Quichean epic tale of "Hunahpu" and "Xbalanque."

In the Classic period of the Maya civilization, the adventures of these two hero twins was common knowledge across the entirety of the Maya area.

The Maya practice of praying to and placing faith into legendary heroes was no different than other religions around the World. In most of the World's religions and faiths, a hero is often sought to bridge the gap between mankind and the gods, much like veneration Catholics showed towards various Saints.

The essential elements of the story of "One Hunahpu," (also called "Ahuapu") the first father, and the miraculous underworld tree were well-known stories among the ancient Maya for many centuries. There have been numerous painted ceramic vases that have been discovered near the ruins of Maya cities in the Yucatan, Guatemala, and Belize depict the great cultural hero confronting the Xibalban Lords of Death. They tell the story of his sacrifice, and display his head hanging in a fruit-laden tree. Ceramics found also depict his eventual resurrection as a maize god of life and abundance.

Although the Popol Vuh's account of 'One Hunahpu' ends with his restoration to life in the underworld, earlier hieroglyphic inscriptions provide us with some additional information.

"Hun-Nal-Ye" was the ancient lowland Maya version of 'One Hunahpu.' Similar to 'One Hunahpu,' the sacrificed 'Hun-Nal-Ye' is displayed in Maya art with his head being hung in a flowering tree in the underworld of Xibalba. He, with the aid of his two sons, was able to arise from the underworld through the cracked shell of a great turtle, which is symbolic in Maya myth of being the earth floating on the surface of the primordial sea.

Hun-Nal-Ye, having been reborn to new life, was then conveyed in a canoe across the sky to the center place of creation. There he oversaw the setting of the sacred three stones. These are the sacred hearthstones of the celestial fire that will stimulate the universe and allow the world to emerge from darkness.

Having completed set the stones, Hun-Nal-Ye then raised the sky above by erecting a great world tree to support the heavens above the world.

According to the writings on the Quirigua Stela C sculpture, erected this creation event took place on the Maya calendar, dated on 13.0.0.0.0 "4 Ahaw 8 Kumk'u" (which is: 13 August 3114 BC). The location that creation took place is called "Lying-Down-Sky, First-Three-Stone-Place" because of it being the location where the sky had once laid unsupported against the World.[271]

Stela C, Quirigua.[270]

Legend states that, "One Hunahpu," (also called "Ahuapu") who is the first father, was walking past the mouth of a cave which led to underworld, known as "Xibalba" (loosely pronounced in English as, "shi-bal-bah").

The gods of the underworld called out to "One Hunahpu" and invited him to come down and play a ball game. He takes the bait and descends into the darkness of the cave where the gods immediately behead him. They then hung "One Hunahpu's" severed head in a calabash tree.

The legend the gives the account of a hero named, "One Hunahpu" who often spent his days playing an ancient Maya ball game with his brother. Unfortunately, the noise they were making while they played the ball game was disturbing the lords of the Xibalba," which happened to be underneath the ball court. The chief lords of the Xiblaba, called "One Death" and "Seven Death," were determined to destroy the brothers and then bring them into their realm of Xibalba.

After a number of attempts, One Death and Seven Death were finally able to overwhelm One Hunahpu. They then sacrificed and beheaded him. One Death and Seven Death buried the headless body of One Hunahpu in the underworld's ball court and placed his head in the fork of an old dead tree. As soon as they placed the head, the tree instantly sprang to life and blossomed a white fruit that resembled the skull of One Hunahpu.

Calabash tree.[272]

The fruit suddenly blooming on the tree amazed the Xibalba lords, 'One Death' and 'Seven Death'. The fruit grew everywhere on the tree and they were no longer sure where the head of 'One Hunahpu' because of the fruit growing all over it. All the Lords of Xibalba seen what was happening to the dead tree and came out to look in amazement.

The lords of the Xibalba were so bewildered and afraid of the power in the tree that they forbade anyone to go anywhere near it. Eventually, word about this wondrous tree and of the sweetness that its fruit possessed had reached the ears of "Xquic," who was the daughter of one of the Xibalba lords. Xquic approached the tree and was about to pick one of the fruits from it when the skull of One Hunahpu spoke to her. The skull warned her to only eat the fruit if she was completely sure of her desire.

She reassured the skull of One Hunahpu that it was indeed her desire to partake in the fruit. However, before she even touched the fruit from the tree, she became miraculously impregnated by a single drop of saliva that One Hunahpu spat into the palm of her hand.

The young woman was then alarmed that by this single act of spitting saliva in her hand that she had miraculously became pregnant. She then climbed out underworld of Xibalba and went up into the world of the living and gave birth to twin sons, Hunahpu and Xbalanque.[271]

The Early Life of the Hero Twins

After the twins, Hunahpu and Xbalanque, were born, they weren't treated very well by their grandmother (One Hunahpu's mother) or elder half-brothers, "One Howler Monkey" and "One Artisan." As soon as they were born, their grandmother demanded they be removed from the house for their crying. The twins elder half brothers were quick to obligate her by placing the newborn twins on an anthill among the thorny brambles. Their intent was to kill the twin newborns out of jealousy and simply out of spite. Before the birth of the twins, elder half brothers had for long time been the ones who were revered as being fine artisans and thinkers. They feared that the newborn twins would steal away their prestige.

Their attempts to murder the young twins right after their birth into this world were a failure and they grew up. During the years of their youth, the twin boys were made to labor and also to hunt birds to bring to for family's meals. Their elder brothers would always be given food to eat first, in spite of them spending the entire day singing and playing while the younger twin boys labored all day.

The twins, Hunahpu and Xbalanque, displayed their wit at a very young age when dealing with their elder half brothers. One day the twins had returned from hunting without any birds for the family to eat and were interrogated by their older siblings over it. The twin boys explained that they did hunt and shoot several birds but the birds they shot were stuck high in a tree and they couldn't retrieve them.

The twins brought their elder brothers to the tree and the elder half brothers then climbed up to fetch the birds. However, while they were climbing the tree suddenly began growing even taller and the older brothers became trapped in it and weren't able to climb down. This was the first known occurrence in which the twins demonstrated any kind of extraordinary powers of any kind.

Hunahpu then embarrassed his elder brethren even more by advising them to remove their pants and tie them around their waists to allow them to climb down from the growing tree. The pants that were tied around the elder brother's waists became tails and they turned into monkeys. When their grandmother found out what happened and that the elder boys hadn't been harmed in any way (except their pride), she demanded that they'd be allowed to return. However, when the elder brothers returned home, the grandmother wasn't able to contain her laughter at how they looked and the disfigured elder brothers fled in shame.

The Defeat of Seven Macaw

Eventually, the twins were approached by the Maya god, "Huracan," regarding an arrogant god named "Seven Macaw" (Vucub Caquix). The Popul Vuh does not specify when this happened, it's assumed during their early adulthood. Seven Macaw had built up a large following of worshipers among some of the inhabitants of the World and had been making false claims that he was either the sun or the moon. Seven Macaw was an extremely vain god who often adorned his wings with metal trinkets and ornaments and would wear a set of teeth that were made from gemstones.

In their first attempt to kill Seven Macaw, the twins attempted to sneak up on him while he was eating his meal in a tree. The twins shot at Seven Macaw's jaw with a blowgun and knocked out of the tree but only wounded.

When the hero twin, Hunahpu tried to escape, the god Seven Macaw grabbed his arm and torn off.

The Hero Twins shooting a perched bird demon "Seven Macaw' with a blowgun. Izapa Stela 25.[174]

Regardless of this failed attempt the hero twins again demonstrated their clever nature by coming up with a plan to defeat the god Seven Macaw. They invoked a pair of deities and disguised them as their 'grandparents.' The hero twins then instructed the invoked deities (who were disguised as their grandparents) to approach Seven Macaw and negotiate for the return of Hunahpu's arm.

The deities disguised as 'grandparents' pleaded that they were just a very poor family and trying to care for their orphaned grandchildren by earning a living as a doctor and dentist. After hearing their pleas, Seven Macaw demands that his teeth be fixed because they'd been shot and knocked loose by the twin's blowgun. He also demanded that his eyes be cured as well (the Popol Vuh does not say what happened to his eyes). The 'grandparents' agreed and replaced his teeth made from gemstones and replaced them with white corn. They then plucked out the ornaments he had for his eyes and left the vain god lacking in his former greatness. The vain god Seven Macaw then died, assumingly from shame.

The Sons of Seven Macaw

"Zipacna" and "Cabrakan," were sons of the vain god Seven Macaw and Chimalmat (a Maya giant). Zipacna and his brother, Cabrakan (meaning: earthquake), were often considered to be demons by the Maya. Zipacna was claimed as not only being vain, but also as being very arrogant and violent.

Zipacna was characterized as a large caiman (an alligatorid crocodilian) and would often boast that he was the creator of the mountains. The elder son of Seven Macaw, Zipacna, was killed when the Hero Twins tricked him with the fake crab lure and then buried him beneath a mountain.

The Popol Vuh tells us the story. One day when Zipacna was basking in the sun while at the beach that he was disturbed by the "Four Hundred Boys" (possibly the Maya gods of alcohol, but this is not certain) who were attempting to construct a hut. They cut down a large tree to use as the main support beam, but weren't able to lift it. Zipacna, who was extremely strong, offered to carry and place the log for them.

The Four Hundred Boys concluded that it wasn't very good that one individual to possess such awesome strength and that Zipacna should be killed because of it. They first tried to trick Zipacna by asking him to dig a hole for their support beam with the intention of thrusting the massive post into the hole while he dug it and thus killing him.

Zipacna was suspicious and realized their deceitful plan in action while he dug the hole and saved himself by covertly digging a side tunnel and hiding inside it when they dropped the heavy post into the hole. To make them think that he'd actually been killed, Zipacna cried out in pain. He then allowed some ants to carry pieces of his hair and some trimmings from his nails out of the hole, making the boys think that he'd been killed.

After three days, the Four Hundred Boys had finished the building their hut and held a celebration. They celebrated, both for completing the hut and for killing Zipacna. They even prepared wine and engaged in drunken festivities.

After the boys had passed out from their drinking, Zipacna emerged the hole and with his colossal strength he knocked over the wooden column and caused their hut to come crashing down upon the boys as they slept, killing the Four Hundred Boys without any survivors. After their death by Zipacna, the Four Hundred Boys entered into the heavens as the open star cluster known as the Pleiades.

"*The Pleiades, also known as the 'Seven Sisters' or, the 'Four Hundred Boys'*" [269]

The Hero Twins, Hunahpu and Xbalanque, had heard what happened to the Four Hundred Boys and decided to exact revenge upon Zipacna for their deaths. This was also part of the Hero Twins goal to bring down the arrogant gods of the Maya. The twins came up with a detailed plan in order to fool and kill Zipacna. They fabricated a life-like faux crab and then concealed it deep within a canyon.

Afterwards they went to the beach and searched for Zipacna, who was hunting for his usual favorite food, crabs. Zipacna was famished and had been unsuccessful in finding any crabs all day. The Hero Twins approached him and told him a very large crab that they'd seen in a canyon.

They guided him to the canyon where they'd seen the alleged crab. Zipacna was so famished that he wasn't able to see through the Twin's ruse and followed them to the canyon. Zipacna seen the crab, not realizing it wasn't real and went into the canyon to fetch it. Suddenly while he was in the canyon, the Twins made *(not specified how)* the mountain come down on him, burying and killing him.

After the death of the strong Zipacna, the god Huracan approached the Hero Twins and asked them for their assistance in dealing with Seven Macaw's other son, Cabrakan (meaning 'the Earthquake').

Once again, the Hero Twins relied on their wits to devise a plan. Cabrakan, like his father and brother, was very proud and arrogant. The Twins decided to use this very arrogance against him. They sought him out and then boasted about a great mountain they'd seen which continued to grow and grow.

Cabrakan was very proud of his ability to bring down mountains. When he heard the Hero Twin speak of this great mountain, as they predicted, he demanded that they show him this mountain. The Hero Twins, Hunahpu and Xbalanque were happy to oblige and escorted Cabrakan on a journey to the mountain (which did not even exist).

Being the skillful hunters that they were, the Twins shot down several birds along the way. Following through with their plan, they stopped and roasted the birds over a fire and played on Cabrakan's hunger. Just as they predicted, being hungry and smelling their food, he asked them for some meat.

The Hero Twins gave him a fake roasted bird which they had secretly fabricated with plaster and gypsum. Upon eating it, he became very weakened from the plaster and gypsum (implying the mixture was poisonous to the gods) and the Hero Twins were able to bind and throw him into a hole deep in the Earth, burying him forever.

Discovery of One Hunahpu's Gaming Equipment

It was some time after the Hero Twins had rid themselves of their elder half brother that they started using their special powers or abilities to facilitate their daily toils for their grandmother. For example, it only took them a single swing of their ax to clear a full day's worth of wood and then they'd relax the remainder of the day.

To keep this a secret from their grandmother, they'd covered themselves in dust and wood chippings to make it appear like they'd been hard at work, when in fact they'd been relaxing. Unfortunately, one day when they returned to work, they discovered that their labors had been all undone by the forest animals.

The Hero Twins decided that they had to do something about this, so when they completed their work for the day, so they hid and patiently waited the animals to return. When the forest animals came back, the twin brothers tried to catch them.

Most of the forest animals were able to avoid being captured by the Twins and easily escaped the brothers. The brothers almost caught the rabbit and deer when they were able to grab their tails; but both the rabbit's and deer's tails broke off, allowing them to escape. The result of losing their tails to the Hero Twins made all future generations of deer and rabbits to have their distinctive short tails.

The brothers did, however, manage to capture the rat. As an act of revenge for undoing their work in the fields, they tortured the rat by singing its tail in a fire. In agony, the rat begged for mercy. The rat promised to reveal some information which would be important to them if they'd release him. The Hero Twins agreed and the rat told them about the ballgame equipment which belonged to their father and uncle that was hidden in the roof of their grandmother's home.

The Twin brothers immediately began devising a plan to get the hidden equipment. When their grandmother cooked hot chili sauce for the evening meal, the Twin brothers snuck the singed tail rat into their home. While they ate, the Twins complained that the chili being too hot and demanded water to drink, which their grandmother left to fetch.

However, the Twins had sabotaged the jar from which she collected the water and she did not return. After a bit, their mother left to find out why grandmother hadn't yet returned with the water. This was when the Twins were finally alone in the home and able to retrieve the hidden items. They sent the singed rat which they smuggled into the home and sent it up into the roof to gnaw apart the ropes that were holding the equipment hidden.

Once the ropes were gnawed through and the Hero Twins were able to recover the hidden ball equipment which belonged to their father and uncle. They used the equipment to play ball, which became their favorite pastime.

275

The Xibalban Ballgames

Having now acquired the ball playing equipment, the Hero Twin brothers, Hunahpu and Xbalanque, played ball in the very same court above Xibalba as had their father and uncle had played in long before them.

When the Hero Twins began playing ball in the court, once again the "Lords of Xibalba" were disturbed by the noise and beckoned the Twins to come to the underworld,"Xibalba," and play in their court.

Afraid her grandsons, the Hero Twins, would suffer the dame fate as her sons did, their grandmother sent a message warning them not to go to Xibalba, but they went anyways.

When their father and uncle had descended into Xibalba, they were met with a number of challenges along the way. These challenges were meant to confuse and embarrass them before they arrived to the ball court. The Hero Twins were determined not going to fall victim to the same tricks. Ahead of them, they sent a mosquito to bite the Lords of the underworld and reveal which were real and which were decoys. They were also able to uncover the identities of each Lord they revealed.

The Xibalban Lords offered a bench for them to sit on, which they claimed was for visitors, but the Twin brother seen through their trick and seen that it was a heated cooking stone. The Xibalbans became frustrated by the Hero Twins' uncanny ability to see through their tricks and traps, so they sent them to the "**Dark House.**" This was the first of several deadly trials that were created by the Lords of Xibalba.

Their father and uncle suffered embarrassing defeats when they went through the trials of the Xibalaban Lords. This was not the case with the Hero Twins, Hunahpu and Xbalanque. They were able to outwit the Xibalbans Lord'se first of the tests by surviving the entire night in the pitch black house without using up their torch.

Frustrated, the Lords of Xibalba bypassed the remaining trials and took the Hero Twins directly to the ball court in Xibalba. The Hero Twins noticed that the Xibalban Lords were using a special bladed ball that was obviously devised to kill them when the twin brother Hunahpu stopped the ball with his playing racket and noticed the blades.

Stopping the game, the Hero Twins threatened to leave because the Xibalban Lords had only summoned them there as a trick to kill them.

The Lords of Xibalba yielded and allowed the Twins to use their own rubber ball and they played a long and proper game. The Hero Twins allowed the Xibalban Lords to win the ball match, but this was also part of their ruse.

They were sent to "**Razor House,**" which was the second deadly trial in the underworld of Xibalba. The Razor House was filled with knives which were animate and able to move on their own. Speaking to the animate knives, the Hero Twins convinced them all to stop moving and ruined the trial. The Hero Twins were also able to convince 'leafcutting ants' to retrieve petals from the gardens of Xibalba to be offered to the Lords of Xibalba as prize for their victory.

The Xibalban Lords intentionally chosen those specific flowers as a victory prize because they thought it would be impossible for the Twins to acquire them. The flowers were well guarded, but the guards did not take notice of the ants sneaking past them. The Lords of Xibalba killed the guards because they had failed to guard the flowers.

The Hero Twins challenged the Lords of Xibalba to a rematch and intentionally lost the game again. This time they were sent to "**Cold House**," which was the next deadly trial. To the dismay of the Lords of Xibalba, the Hero Twins easily defeated this trial as well.

Again the Hero Twins played a ball game against the Lords of Xibalba and again lost on purpose in oder to be sent to the remaining deadly trials: "**Jaguar House**," "**Fire House**," and "**Bat House**." Each of which they defeated in each trial designed by the Lords of Xibalba.

The Lords of Xibalba were getting more and more frustrated at the them successfully defeating the deadly trials until the Hero Twins, Hunahpu and Xbalanque, were placed in the "Bat House." Though the Twin brothers hid inside their blowguns from the deadly bats, Hunahpu had peeked out of his blowgun to see if daylight had arrived yet and was immediately decapitated by one of the deadly bat.

The Lords of Xibalba were overjoyed by defeating Hunahpu and killing him. The surviving Hero Twin,

Xbalanque, summoned one of the beasts of the field and fashioned a 'replacement head' for his brother Hunahpu.

Hunahpu's decapitated head was used as the playing ball in the next day's game. It was during that game that the Hero Twins were able to secretly substitute a squash or gourd for the playing ball and retrieved Hunahpu's real head, which resulted in an embarrassing defeat for the Lords of Xibalbans.

Downfall of Xibalba

Embarrassed by their defeat the Lords of Xibalba were determined more than ever to destroy the Hero Twins. The Xibalban Lords had a great oven built and then summoned the Hero Twins with the intent of tricking them into the oven and burning them to their deaths. The Hero Twins knew that the Lords of Xibalba were leading them into a trick, but allowed themselves to be tricked into the oven, burned, and then have their bones ground into dust.

The Lords of Xibalba were estatic by their victory in finally destroying the Twins. They took their ashes and cast them into a river. However, this was all a part of the plan devised by the Hero Twins as they were hoping the Xibalban Lords would cast them into the river. When the ashes of the Hero Twins were cast into the river, their bodies began to regenerate. First they regenerated as catfish until they finally regenerated back as a pair of young twin boys once again, but looking slightly different.

Not recognizing the twin boys, the Hero Twins were allowed to remain among the Xibalbans. Stories about their transformation from catfish to boys spread, as well as stories about their dancing and how they entertained the people of Xibalba. The boys performed a number of miracles by setting fire to buildings and then bringing them back whole from burnt ashes. They would also sacrifice each another and then raise each other from the dead.

When the Lords of Xibalba heard these stories, they summoned the twins to their court in order to entertain them, demanding to see the rumored miracles for themselves.

The twin boys obligated the Lords of Xibalba, as their real identities were unknown to the Xibalban Lords for the moment. When questioned who they were, the Twins claimed to be orphans and vagabonds and the Lords of Xibalba were none the wiser.

The Twins went through their series of miracle performances by slaying a dog and bringing it back from the dead. They caused the Xibalban Lords house to burn around them while those inside were left completely unharmed. After which, they brought the house back to whole from the burnt ashes. As a grand finale, Xbalanque cut his twin brother Hunahpu apart and offered him up as a sacrifice, only to have his dead brother rise, complete and whole once again from the dead.

The Lords of Xibalba were so impressed by the performance that the highest lord of Xibalba , One Death and Seven Death demanded that the twin boys perform the miracle on them. The twins obliged by killing the highest Xibalban lords and offered them as a sacrifices. However, the Twins refused resurrect the slayed high lords back from the dead.

At this point, the Hero Twins then shocked the Xibalbans by revealing their real identities as being Hunahpu and Xbalanque, sons of One Hunahpu, whom the Lords of Xibalba had slain years ago along with their uncle

Seven Hunahpu. The Xibalbans, now in despair, confessed to the crimes of killing the brothers years ago and begged the Hero Twins for mercy.

As a punishment for their crimes of murdering their father and uncle, the underworld realm of Xibalba was no longer allowed to exist as place of head in great honor and the Xibalbans would no longer receive offerings from the people who walked on the Earth above them.

The Hero Twins had effectively defeated the underworld of Xibalba.

Death and ascension of Hunahpu and Xbalanque

Now that the underworld realm of Xibalba had been defeated and the arrogant gods were disposed of, the Hero Twins Hunahpu and Xbalanque still had one final act to complete. They returned to the Xibalban ball-court and dug up the buried remains of their father, One Hunahpu and attempted to resurrect him.

The Twins managed to make his body whole again, but their father was no longer the same and wasn't unable to function as he had once before. The Hero Twins left their father there in the ball-court, but before leaving they told him that he'd be prayed to by those who were seeking hope and that eased their father's heart.

Having completed their quest, the Hero Twins departed the underworld of Xibalba and returned to the surface of Earth. Continued their ascent and continued climbing all the way up into the sky and became the Sun and Moon.

Their father, One Hunahpu, was following them up to the surface of the earth and seen corn growing along the way. He harvested an ear of corn and became the "God of

Maize."

The belief of all ancient Maya was that they're the direct descendants of that one ear of corn. This is the core definition to the Maya people of who is Maya and who is not. The descendants of the first ear of corn picked by the God of Maize, One Hunahpu.

Chapter 16

Maya Society and Life

Maya society was no different than any other society around the world during this time period. Their society was broken into a class structure, which followed how other civilizations were. You had the ruling class, the nobility ("almehenob"), the priesthood ("ahkinob") and often scribes would be at this level as well, the common folk ("ah chembal uinieol"), and of course, the slaves ("pencatob").

The most powerful of the ruling elite was known as the "halach uinic" or "true man," which makes a fifth class in some cases.

The halach uinic (Chief or King) was a hereditary position that was typically passed from father to eldest son. Really no different than the customs practiced in Europe and Asia. However, when no suitable heir was available, a council of lords would elect a successor from the noble families.

The halach uinic (king) was a despotic position and it held ultimate political authority over the entire city-state they ruled. The halach uinic also saw to civil affairs and relations with neighboring city-states. So revered was the halach uinic, that a cloth was held in front of his face to prevent anyone from speaking to him directly.

HM 1172: Palace Scene. 600-900 AD, Mexico. This cacao server has a ruler seated tailor fashion on a throne and surrounded by three attendants; two are armed. The ruler wears an elaborate headdress, ear ornaments, a plaque with attachments and jaguar leggings. The attendants wear distinctive headgear representing three different animals.
[232]

It was the wealthy Maya aristocracy that made up the nobility. Of this class of nobles, the 'halach uinic' would select provincial managers or governors that were known as "batabs." These batabs assisted the ruling halach uinic with local governments and would see to the required payment of tributes (taxes) to the ruler(s).

During the Maya Classic Period, the typical small kingdom (ajawil, ajawlel, ajawlil) was ruled by a hereditary ruler called an "Ajaw" (later "k'uhul Ajaw"). An Ajaw or Ahau ('Lord') is a political title attested from the epigraphic inscriptions of the pre-Columbian Maya civilization.

Ajaw is also the 20th named day on the tzolk'in (divinatory calendar) when an Ajaw's (ruler) was required to fulfill the k'atun-ending rituals. These rituals fell upon the leader and required ritualistic self sacrifice, usually in the form of bloodletting.

The use and meaning of "Ajaw" was used generically for "lord", "ruler", "king" or "leader", which meant any of the leading or ruling class of nobles. However, it was not limited to a single individual, as rule of a given was sometimes shared. Additionally, because the Ajaw performed religious activities, the title was not only given to the ruler, but also to a designated member of the locality or city-state's priesthood.

The variation of ajaw is the "kuhul ajaw," ("divine lord") which is the title for a sovereign leader of a given kingdom or city-state. Even though the extent of the territory that was controlled by an ajaw varied considerably and the title could also be for individuals, who in theory, recognized the lordship over another person, dynasty, kingdom, or city-state. Ajaw was used by the Maya as Lord was used by the Europeans as a title for anyone that had any kind of authority over you.

The title of Ajaw was also given to women, although it

was generally prefixed with the sign "Ix" ("woman") to indicate gender, such as: Ix ajaw.

In the Maya hieroglyphics writing system, the representation of the word "ajaw" could be as either a character or symbol, or it could be spelled-out using syllables (A-jaw).

Maya logogram of Tzolkin Day 20 "Ajaw."[1227]

The term Ajaw (or Ahau) appears in many early Colonial texts where writers used it as a generic synonym when they were referring to rulers and their domains. It was used when referring to the rulers or leaders that were Aztec, Maya, or Spanish without any discrimination of culture.

Another reference for leader used in many of the writings during the Spanish colonization were the words 'tlatoani' and 'tlahtocayotl.' These words came from the Nahuatl language of the Aztecs. Nevertheless, some of Spanish chroniclers used them interchangeably when referring to the Maya and any other Mesoamerica rulers.

The word Tlatoani (which literally means "speaker") was the Nahuatl term for the ruler of an altepetl, which was an Aztec state before the Spanish Conquistadors. Similar to the Mayan language adding the prefix Ix to Ajaw, the Aztec Nahuatl language added a prefix signifying female gender, using cihuā-tlàtoāni for a female ruler or queen. The term 'cuauh-tlatoani' refered to a provisional, interim, or a non-dynastic ruler. The ruler's lands were called 'tlahtohcātlālli' and the ruler's house was called 'tlahtohcācalli.'[228][229][230][231]

Such petty kingdoms were usually nothing more than small city-states made up of a main capital and some surrounding villages or towns. Although the Maya were not an empire like the Aztecs, but instead a collection a small city-state like kingdoms like the Greeks; there were some very large entities that controlled larger territories and subjugated smaller kingdoms under their rule. An example of such larger and more extensive political systems would be like those controlled by the kingdoms of Tikal and Caracol.

Most kingdoms subjugated under another kingdom often remained intact as a political entity as well. Withstanding the constant warfare and occasional shifts in regional power, most kingdoms never disappeared from the political landscape until the collapse of the whole system in the 9th century AD.

Classic Maya societies put an emphasis on the centrality of the royal household, especially towards the ruler of that household. Most kingdoms were built around the ruling house. Spanish sources invariably describe even the largest

Maya settlements of Yucatán and Guatemala areas as being dispersed collections of dwellings that were grouped around the temples and palaces of the ruling dynasty or nobles.

Some researchers argue that Maya cities were structured in such a way that were not actually meant be urban centers; but more to meet the needs of the enormous royal households when they conducted their administrative and ritual activities in the royal courts. These courts held the priesthood as well as the nobility, as their court functions often went hand in hand.

Scribes also held a prominent position in Maya royal courts. They even had their own patron deities, such as the Howler Monkey Gods and Maya maize god.

The Maize God as scribe.[121]

Howler monkey statue, temple 11, Copan.[120]

Considered a prestigious position, most scribes are likely to have come from families of the aristocracy. But writing was not practiced exclusively by scribes. Maya art often depicts rulers as having pen bundles in their headdresses or having some other writing tool, such as a shell or clay ink-pot. This indicated that they were either scribes or at least able to read and write.

Maya priests also held a very high position in society. They not only performed their religious duties, but priests also acted as administrators, scholars, astronomers, and mathematicians. The priesthood carried as much prestige, power, and influence over the Maya people as the noble class. Priests were both feared and respected for their knowledge and position before the gods. Like in all other religions, opportunistic priests were able to extort the superstitions of the people for their own advantage and gain.

The Maya priesthood also provided high status positions for those descendants of nobility who were not able to obtain a political office or position. If one could not achieve power through the throne, they definitely could through the sacrificial altar.

Maya priests were usually the sons of priests or the second sons of nobles and were usually trained through an apprentice system which consisted of a hierarchy of professional priests who served as intermediaries between the kingdom's population and the deities. This was when an apprentice priest would learn basic skills, such as the art of reading and writing.

The priesthood as a whole were the keepers of knowledge concerning the beliefs and practices. This included their calendars and astrological calculations, divination, prophecies. They also kept the knowledge to interpret spiritual omens that would predict future events. In addition, the Maya priests were experts in historiography and maintained the genealogical records.[154]

Among the duties of the priesthood was human sacrifice. This was a rite performed by a priest who was called the "nacom." or "ah nakom." The status of this priest was relatively low and it was a position which meant for life. It was the nacom whose duty it was to cut the hearts out of the sacrificial victims during human sacrificial ceremonies and rituals. This is in contrast to the film "Apocalypto" where the nacom was portrayed as being the high priest.

The Maya high priests were called "ahau can mai" or

simply as "ah kin mai." The end word of their title after 'ahau can' or 'Ah kin' being either their own family name ('mai") or that of a functional designation within larger kingdoms.

The town priests were called the "ah k'in," which basically translates as: 'diviner.' With the "k'in" in the priest's title "ah k'in" meaning 'sun' or 'day', essentially means loosely as, 'diviners of the sun'.

The local 'ah k'in' had the responsibility of conducting public and private rituals within individual towns throughout the province. They preached about the ancestors and deities to the masses and published the festival days that needed to be observed. It was also their job to determine the appropriate rituals and sacrifices that needed to be administered.

These ah k'in, or town priests, were also usually assisted by four old men who were called 'chac'. The priests who had a very influential role in their duties were the oracles known as "chilan" or "chilam." It is said that the chilan may have used mind-altering substances to assist them in making their prophecies.

Maya priestly functions were often fulfilled by nobles and not by a professional class of priests. The sovereignty was considered a religious institution and the temple's service was the sacred duty of the sovereign. During certain intervals of the sacred calendars, Maya rulers would often abstain from intercourse while they fasted, prayed, and burnt offerings, pleading to the gods for the sun's light and for the lives of their vassals and servants.

The highest Maya nobility is stated to have served continually in the temple, whereas there is no regular priest mentioned. It was possibly the chiefs and kings who performed the priestly functions themselves in many cases. The Yucatec king was called the "halach uinic" ('true man'), is characterized as being both 'ruler' and 'high priest.'

During the Classic period, the Maya ruler was most of a priestly king, often assuming the priesthood as a whole. Notwithstanding the existence of a separate priesthood, which indeed existed in most kingdom's courts, towns, and local villages.

While the ruling nobility and priesthood sat comfortably at the top of the Maya social class system, the commoners and slaves sat at the bottom. These were the masses who were subjects under the rule of the nobles and priests. These were the common people who spent their lives as hunters, farmers, sand builders. These were the subjugated commoners who toiled to support not only themselves but also those above them.

The lowest class of people in Maya society were the slaves. The source of Maya slaves most oftenly came from prisoners of war, orphans, and the children of slaves. The Maya also made slaves out of criminals, such as those who were caught stealing or committing any other crime not punishable by death.

Slavery was not always a permanent predicament, as the Maya would often follow a custom which allowed for the possibility of paying a ransom for the release of a slave.

Nevertheless, as it was the common way which was

practiced by the rest of the world, a slave was considered property and their fate was at the mercy of their owners.

Maya Houses

For the most part, the architectural splendor of the Maya civilization can be accredited to that of the common man. Their building ingenuity started at the lowest level, in the construction of their very own homes. The Maya built their houses with very steep roofs that were made of thatch or palm leaves. This prevented the rain from getting through and into the house.

Their roofs were also made to drop very low in the fronts in order to protect the inhabitants inside against the hot sun and rains. These low dropped roofs also helped the inhabitants to better defend themselves from enemies as well.

They also built a wall that ran lengthwise, dividing the whole house. They also placed doorways in the back of the house, where they had their beds and slept. Their beds were made of small rods that were covered with weaved grass mats and mantles of cotton that was used as covering. During the summer time when it was hot, they sleep on mats in the front part of the house. This was especially true with the men in the household.

The front half of their houses were whitened with a very fine whitewash. There is no known reason for this other than the assumption of for looks, but may have also been to help strengthen the front of the house walls, which were probably wattle and daub styled walls.

The front whitewashed portion of the house also served as the reception and lodging area for guests and visitors. The were no doors on the fronts of the houses. There was no real fear of crimes being committed with the houses being door-less, open and unsecured. Maya society held it as being a grave offense to do any wrong to another's house.[138]

Thatched roof building, Source: William Gates, p32. 1937. [138]

The ruler or noble's house was usually built at the expense of the common man or subject *(nothing has changed for thousands of years anywhere in humankind)*. These houses that the commoners had built for the noble class, or chiefs of their village, were often equipped with beautiful frescoes as well.

Body Modifications

The Maya people who lived in the Yucatan were described as being a tall and robust people of good physique who possessed great strength. They were also described as having a common feature of being bow-legged as well. This was a desired trait and it's speculated as having been caused from being carried astride their mother's hip since infancy. At least, this was what was practiced by the Maya in order to achieve this trait.

Another highly desired trait was to be cross-eyed (strabismus). Maya mothers who would suspend an object between the eyes of their infants in an attempt to artificially induce the desired crossed-eyed trait. Having crossed eyes was considered honoring "Kinich Ahau," the cross-eyed Maya Sun god, in order to appease and gain his favor. Because of this, it was also considered a god-like handsome trait as well.

The Noble class often had the top of their heads or foreheads flattened when they were infants. This practice was performed by their mothers who would strap boards on the heads of their babies to flatten their foreheads.

This physical trait was considered to be a lifelong sign of noble status.[276] It is not known if commoners practiced this form of status body mutilation.

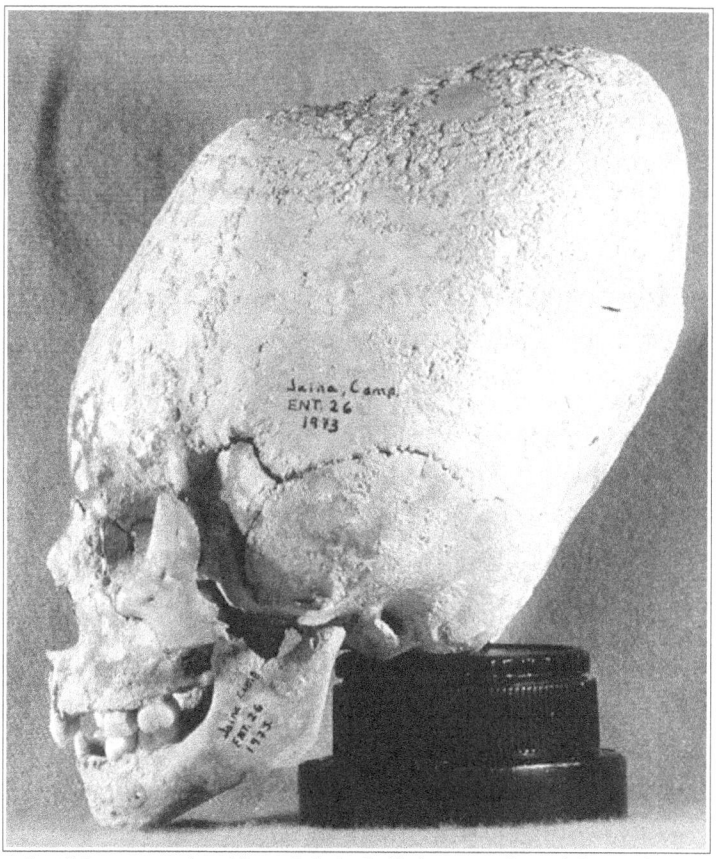

The ancient Maya pressed and bound their skulls into a variety of shapes that probably reflected an individual's place in society.[276][277]

The Maya also pierced their ears and adorned them with a variety of styles of earrings, plugs, and other ear pieces. It was also noted that their bodies were very scarified from making bloodletting self sacrifices to appease their deities and ancestors. This was especially true of the nobles and heads of households.

The Maya men did not grow beards and they claim that their mothers used to burn their faces with hot cloths when they were boys as to prevent the growth of any bearding.

When beards were grown by Maya men, they were very rough, much like bristles of a boar. Grown men either burned off or used tweezers to pluck out all of their facial hair.

Both Maya men and women of all classes plucked out or burned off their eyebrows as well. Facial hair wasn't regarded as very desirable trait and wasn't considered to be fashionable. In retrospect of this, there are some earlier murals that depict some Maya rulers who would occasionally have mustaches and/or beards.

Both Maya men and women allowed their hair to grow out fully, often binding it at the top with a ring. This form of hair binding allowed the hair to grow long below. but remain short on the crown. Some kept it braided and wound around their head with an end left behind like a queue.

The Maya used mirrors and kept themselves carefully groomed and decorated. A vanity that has long been a part of their lives as ground and polished stone mirrors date back to 1500 BC in Mesoamerica. They were usually made from a mosaic of iron pyrite pasted onto wood, slate or other material and then polished to a mirror like finish.

There are also some depictions of the Classic-era Maya royal court which often show their rulers gazing into mirrors.

Scene from a painted vase, a lord gazes at a small effigy mirror-bearer.[268]

Much as the Vikings were known for, the Maya bathed a great deal. They were not modest while they bathed either, as they couldn't be bothered enough to cover themselves before their women, except such as one might do with their hand.

Both the men and women were devoted to various scents and perfumes. They often had bouquets of flowers and other odorous plants arranged about with much care given. Their strategic placement could even be considered as artful.

The Spanish colonial observer also noted that Maya men and women also painted their faces and entire bodies red. Having painted your face and body entirely red was considered as being handsome.[138]

Some of the Maya tattooed their bodies and are

considered as being very valiant and brave when they have many of these tattoos, as the process is very painful. When receiving a tattoo, the craftsman first covers the part he wishes with color and then will meticulously pierce the pictures into the person's skin with delicate precision. Their method is so the blood and color leave the outline of the tattoo on the body.

On account of the pain, the tattooing is done in small sessions. Many times the tattoo location will also fester with infection.

They go through all this to be tattooed and then ridicule those who are not tattooed as being too cowardly to receive them.

The Maya women will tattoo their bodies from the waist up, often leaving their breasts not tattooed for nursing reasons (and possibly due to high pain sensitivity). The patterns they had tattooed on their upper bodies would also be more delicate and beautiful than those possessed by the men.

Examples of head dress and facial scarring and tattooing.[266]

The ancient Maya people also placed a high value on certain extreme body modifications. They often went through very tedious and painful procedures as a rite of passage into manhood or when becoming a warrior or hunter. Sometimes modifications or scarring was done to pay homage to their gods or ancestors. Often these body modifications was done in order to be permanent and visible status symbols tied the individual's place in Maya society. These marks of status that would last throughout their lifetimes and into their afterlife when they joined their ancestors.

Another physical feature which was also practiced by Vikings and early Norse warriors on another part of the World, was to have their teeth sharpened. Some Maya warriors would have their teeth filed down to very sharp points to give them a very fierce appearance and mark status of a warrior. This was often done by adolescent warriors when their permanent teeth were grown in as a rite of passage and form of acceptance amongst the older warriors.

Some upper class women often had their teeth drilled with holes and then had the holes filled in with different decorations made from various gems, such as jadeite, hematite, pyrite, and turquoise for example.

Diego de Landa (second Bishop of the Spanish controlled Yucatan) wrote this account while he was in Maya country in the year 1566 AD. He also referred to the custom among some of the women of filing the teeth like a saw, which they considered to be ornamental and beautiful.
[93][138]

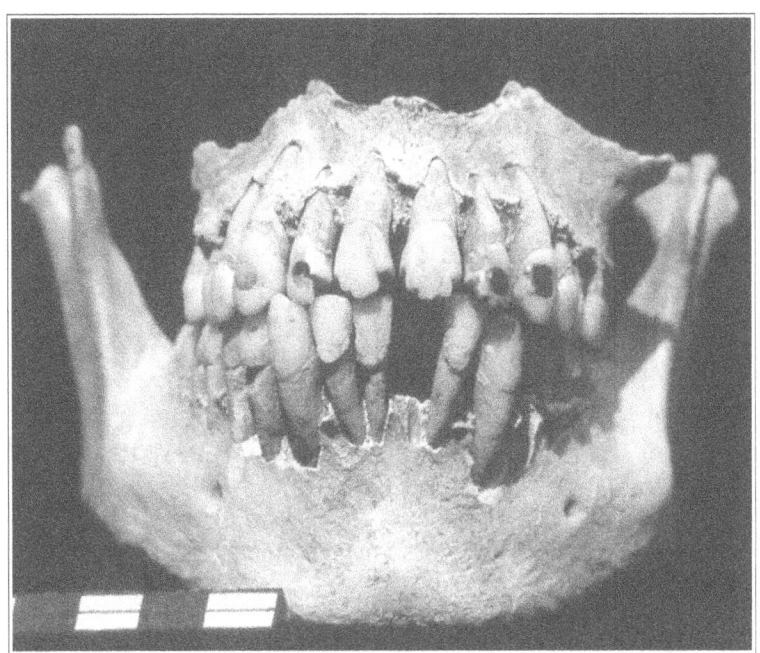

Ancient Maya of all social classes filed their teeth in decorative patterns, but jade inlays were usually reserved for the elites.[276][278]

Bishop Diego also described the Maya clothing of the men as being a strip of cloth which was as broad (wide) as a person's hand in which they wrapped several times about their waist, leaving one end hang in front and one behind.

These ends would be embroidered by their wives with much care and feather work added. He said that they also wore large square mantles, which they threw over their shoulders. On their feet, they wore sandals made from of hemp or deerskin which was tanned dry and then no other garments.[138]

Portrait of Nezahualpilli, king of Tezcoco, attributed to Ixtlilxochitl, although Mexican, illustrates well the garments here described. William Gates, [1937] pg.33.[138]

Besides body modification, body painting was a common practice with the Maya. Several Classic period murals and vases have depictions of warriors with their bodies painted either red or black. These men often painted their bodies and faces like this in order to look fiercer as warriors.

Maya women painted their bodies red in order to look more beautiful. Small paint jars of red hematite mixed with mica have been found in houses in Ceten by archaeologists to confirm this practice. The men who were not married would paint their bodies black, as did those whom were purifying themselves and fasting for rituals. Priests often wore the color famously known as, "Maya Blue."[265]

Sacred Colors

The ancient Maya believed that certain colors were important and had significant spiritual meaning behind them. They believed that these specific colors represented the "Four Cardinal Directions" (North, East, South and West) as well as representative to the various gods within their complex religious belief system.

Each direction had various items within their respective color that were associated with it as well. These items were often included with sacrifices to represent their color, the associated gods, and sacred direction.

According to the Book of Chilam Balam;

- The color **red** represented the East and the gods "Ix Noh Uc, Ox Tocoy-moo, Ox Pauah Ek and Ah Miz." All things which were the color red represented the East and its associated gods.

  East was the most important direction since it's where the Sun's born. The Maya concept of direction, East not North, would always be at the top of maps. East was the primary sacred direction.

- The color **white** represented the North and the gods

"Batun, Ah Puch, Balam-na and Ake." The people in the North had sacred items that were all white.

The North was referred as being the 'side of heaven' because it was direction from where the cooling rains of winter originated. Additionally, this is the direction of the north star which the sky pivoted around.

- **Black** was the color that represented the sacred direction West and the gods "Iban, Ah Chab, and Ah Tucuch." The people in the West presented sacred items which were black in color

  The West was considered the dying place of the Sun when it left us and ended the day.

- The color **yellow** represented the South and the gods "Ah Yamas, Ah Puc, Cauich, and Ah Couoh." The People in the South had sacred items which were yellow.

  The South was considered to be the right-hand or the great side of the Sun.

The fifth color that was associated with the Maya concept of heaven, earth, and the underworld was the color blue-green. This color was found in the center of the four cardinal directions, running vertically from the underworld to the heavens. This direction also had its respective sacred ceiba tree, bird, bean, and corn and united the four cardinal directions with the layers of heaven and the underworld.

In the paintings and murals that cover the walls of the ancient pyramids, many of these sacred colors have been found in the Yucatan in ancient Maya cities. The sacred colors have also been seen in the fragments of clothing that have been found among the buried dead. Additionally on the various glazed pots and jugs which were found buried with these people as well.[273]

The most sacred color to the ancient Maya is a color that is named "Maya Blue." This color was first identified in the year 1931 AD and is a light blue pigment that has puzzled archaeologists, chemists, and various material scientists for years. This color pigment used by the ancient Maya has an unusual chemical stability and composition, It is also a very persistent color which is able to maintain in one of the world's harshest climates.

However, anthropologists have recently discovered how the ancient Maya produced this unusual and widely studied blue pigment.

The Maya city site of the pyramid in Chichén Itzá is one of the Seven Wonders of the Ancient World. It is an extremely important pre-Columbian archaeological site which had been built by the Maya who were living on what is now the Yucatán Peninsula of Mexico. It the beginning of the 20th century, when the Sacred Cenote Well at Chichén Itzá was dredged, the presence of a 14-foot layer of blue precipitate was discovered at the bottom of the sacred well.

Blue was the color of sacrifice for the ancient Maya. Priest wore this color and they painted human beings blue before thrusting them backwards on an altar and cut their beating hearts from their bodies. The victims of human sacrifice were also painted blue before they were thrown into the Sacred Cenote located at Chichén Itzá.

Additionally, this shade of blue was used on painted murals, pottery, and other items that were thrown into the well to appease the gods.

Mural depicting ancient Maya heart extraction at Chichén Itzá.[1112]

The renowned sacrificial color to the Maya was paint color "Maya Blue." This color, which was only known to the ancient Maya, was an important and vivid color which was a virtually indestructible pigment. The color pigment is resistant to age and weather fading, various acids, and even modern chemical solvents which deteriorate any other color pigment.

The color pigment 'Maya Blue' is hailed as being one of the great technological and artistic achievements to come out of Mesoamerica.

Researchers have long known that the remarkably stable Maya Blue pigment is a result from a unique chemical bond with indigo and an unusual clay minerals which has long interior channels called palygorskite.

Several experiemtns have discovered that Maya Blue can be created by heating a mixture of the clay mineral palygorskite with a small amount of indigo. However researchers haven't been able to figure out how the ancient Maya actually produced the color pigment themselves.

New research has revealed that at the site at Chichén Itzá, the creation of "Maya Blue" was resultant as part of the of the rituals that were performed alongside the Sacred Cenote well. The Maya were known to use indigo, copal incense, and the clay palygorskite for medicinal purposes. These three healing items were combined and heated with fire during the ritual the was performed at the edge of the Sacred Cenote. The end result of this ritual produced the pigment of "Maya Blue."

Sacrifices were then painted with paint made from this pigment of blue and then were thrown into the Sacred Cenote Well with the intention of pleasing the rain god "Chaak."

Rain was critical to the ancient Maya people who lived in the northern Yucatan. It hardly rained during the dry season which usually ran from the month of January to mid-May. Offerings of these three healing elements of indigo, copal, and palygorskite was believed to feed the rain god Chaak and bring him into the ritual in hopes that he'd bring rainfall and allow the corn to grow again. [111]

Chapter 17

Maya Weapons and Warfare

At the beginning of the 20th century. the ancient Maya were often idealized as being a predominantly peaceful society. A Mesoamerican indigenous culture focused primarily on philosophy and astronomy. Because the Maya were not a centralized, conquering empire such as the Aztec, it was idealized that they were much like the idealized misconception of the Greeks. A collection of peaceful city-states full of philosophers and artists. They tend to forget the Spartans were Greeks too.

The view of the Maya being the noble savage eventually shifted when detailed analysis of iconography and script deciphering by researchers revealed a very different society. A society that did war and were at times even more brutal than what the Aztec were believed to be.

This spawned the belief that regional warfare was the cause of the collapsing of the Maya civilization which led to the abandonment of entire cities which are now ruins scattered in Mesoamerican jungles.

There were many reasons for the collapse of the Maya civilization prior to the arrival of the Spanish. As always, warfare certainly played a role, but problematic overpopulation which eventually led to environmental degradation of agricultural lands. Mix in some serious natural disasters such as devastating hurricanes on the coastal regions and droughts inland, they all played major roles in the decline of Maya society.

Deeper investigation has revealed that long-term warfare was evidently limited during the Classic Period of Maya history. Nevertheless, militarism was clearly a very prevalent and important ritualistic activity that was deeply rooted in Maya culture. Most of the warfare engaged was emphasized more on territorial control which gave rise to blood feuds between neighboring clans. However, the skirmishes were generally on a smaller scale and battles fought mostly during raids by or on enemy camps.

The is also speculation that the need for sacrificial victims to appease the gods or requirement for slaves required for large construction projects may have been some of the reasoning behind the raids and unannounced attacks on each other's realms.

At some sites , such as those in Tikal and Seibal, it has been discovered by archaeologists that defense barriers were built such as walls and other barricades around the city. It has also been found that during the Classic Period, guerrilla warfare techniques were also heavily utilized in some defensive methods which included the use of palisades, thorn entanglements, and dead-fall traps.

HM 626: Kneeling Warrior with Shield. 600-900 AD, Mexico. Palmer Collection.[233]

Maya warriors were usually equipped with spears, clubs, knives, and shields for hand-to-hand combat. During the Post-classic period, influences from the north introduced 'atlatls' (spear-throwers) to their arsenal of weaponry. The primary goal of Maya warfare, or any warfare in Mesoamerica in general, wasn't to kill or destroy your enemy. The main goal was to capture as many of the enemy's warriors and leaders as possible.

The captives with elite status were the most coveted because they typically became the subjects for human sacrifice to thank the gods for victory and other favor. The captured commoner warriors were usually killed or sentenced to a life of slavery.

There are depictions on painted murals and reliefs, such as the ones at Bonampak and on other Maya artifacts, which illustrate many rituals that were accompanied by the act of war. The Maya had rituals and ceremonies that were held in honor of specific gods in hopes of gaining their support or blessing for battle. The shields and weapons of the Maya warriors were also decorated with symbols of these war gods.

Warriors also ornamented themselves with headdresses, jade earspools, lip plugs, and necklaces. They wore capes made from jaguar skin and body paint indicating their social-economic status and position of power.

They dressed in their best and in their fiercest. The fierce-looking battle attire dawned on by these warriors was meant to terrify their enemies and bring fear to the supernatural forces that opposed them.

These decorated warriors would then be led into battle by horns, drums, whistles, and voice commands while they followed the magnificently feathered banner of their war band.

Maya Ruler, Warrior, and Peasant Levy. Illustrator: Angus McBride.[67]

Warfare has often been employed against competitive rivalries throughout the history of Maya culture for the sole purpose of obtaining sacrificial victims. It was also used to settle disputes with their neighbors and to acquire needed resources critical to their own realm.

Warfare was not only important, but critical to the Maya religion. Raids on neighboring clans and their surrounding areas provided them with the necessary victims required for human sacrifice, as well as slaves for the construction of temples.

This may have been the reasoning behind why the Maya never expanded into a vast empire such as the Aztec. The Maya's petty kingdoms and small city-states allowed for constant small scale off and on warfare to acquire captives.

Large-scale battles were also fought to determine control of territories in order to secure economic power and gain control of important trade routes.

These large scale battles pushed the Maya to defend their cities with very elaborate defensive structures. Some cities built a wall within the outer wall, so advancing enemies would be trapped between the two walls and could be slaughtered in great number.

During the end of the Classic period the amount of internal warfare intensified significantly as the Maya became more and more splintered politically. Maya forces became enlarged to the point that mercenaries were hired. The resultant destruction of many urban city centers from these large scale wars helped contribute to the decline of the Maya.

The battle organization the Maya following this typical set up: The ruler of a Maya city was the supreme war captain. This ruler would form a militia from within their realm. The militia units were then headed by hereditary war chiefs, called "nacoms," These nacoms would employed ritual as well as strategic tactics in their warfare. Some 'nacoms' were only chief war strategists and their troops were led into battle by "batabs," or officers.[122]

Stela 5 at Uaxactun depicts a Tikal lord, Smoking-Frog, as the aggressor in the conflict between the two city-states.

However, these large scale militias weren't always employed en mass. The Mesoamerica jungle terrain made it difficult for large armies to maneuver and control. The defending warriors who were familiar to the landscape of the battlefield were able to strategically maneuver in the familiar wilderness.

The weaponry utilized by the Maya included missile weapons, such as spear-throwers known as atlatls, blowguns, obsidian tipped arrows, although it's been reported that bows were not used that extensively. Hand to hand weapons included obsidian spiked clubs, spears, axes, and knives. All bladed with either knapped chert or obsidian pieces.

Occasionally there were few warrior who wore helmets, but decorative headdresses were more popularly worn on the head. Many warriors bore decorated shields that were made from woven mats of wood with dried animal skins to protect themselves with.

The Maya war leaders dressed elaborately to inspire the warriors following them into battle and bring terror to their enemies. These leaders usually wore padded cotton armor which had a mantle with various religious insignia on it. They also wore very elaborate wooden, animal skin, and cloth headdresses which represented the animal spirit of the deity that supported them, usually a jaguar. Weapons and arms made from metal, as was typical with Europeans, was not used in warfare because of the limited supply and lack of developed forging techniques.[123][124]

The Spanish described the weapons that were used by the Petén Maya as being: bows and arrows, fire-sharpened poles, flint-headed spears, and two-handed swords known as "hadzab."

The hadzab was crafted from strong wood with twin jagged blades which were fashioned from sharp obsidian insets along the edges, similar to the Aztec macuahuitl.[65]

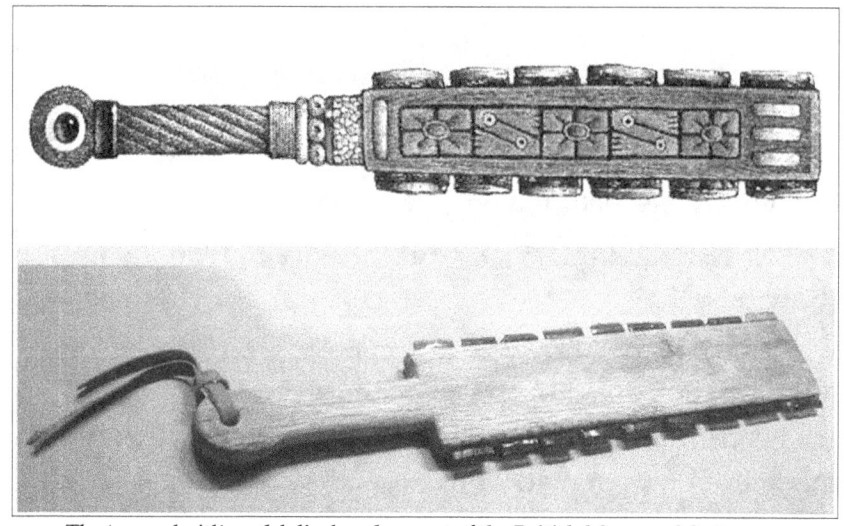

The 'macuahuitl' model displayed as part of the British Museum Moctezuma exhibition, London (bottom); artist's impression by Felipe Dávalos (top).[66]

Even though the Maya had and utilized missile technology, such as bows and arrows, the atlatl, blowguns and spear, most combat occurred at close range with hand to hand weapons. Missile weapons were not heavily relied upon because the goal was not to kill your enemy, but capture him if you could.

Weapons that were used by the Maya were crafted mostly from materials such as obsidian and chert, instead of metal. Metal was known, but not yet found to be useful in the region in lieu of other materials such as obsidian.

The obsidian they used was very, very sharp but also very brittle as well. The Maya would knap pieces of chert or obsidian into projectile points and then attach them to the the ends of their atlatl darts, spear shafts, or arrows. This was the dominant technology in the entire Mesoamerican region.[113]

When the Spanish Conquistadors arrived with their iron armor and arms, the Maya weren't totally defenseless against them. The warrior's weapon of choice against the armored Spaniards was the spear throwing atlatl.

An atlatl (or ahtlatl) was a tool that used leverage to achieve greater velocity in dart or spear throwing. It consists of a shaft with a cupped or spurred end that supports the butt of a dart or spear in order to propel it.

The dart used, called a "yaomitl" in Mayan, is much more like an arrow in design than the darts that were used by early Eurasians. Like an arrow, it had flexible fletching at the end of the dart to stabilize its flight through the air. The darts were made in variety lengths, depending on its usage.

The atlatl was relatively simple to use. It is held in one hand and gripped near the end of the tool farthest from the cup. A dart or short spear butt is set in the end of the cup, aligned with the tool. The dart is then thrown by the swinging action of the upper arm and wrist working together with the atlatl acts as a lever.

The atlatl becomes a low-mass and fast-moving extension of the throwing arm with the increased length of the lever. The lever's extra length allowed the dart or spear thrower to increase force of energy to the spear or dart over a greater distance. This increased the energy of thrust force and ultimately propelled the dart or spear at higher speeds. This made the weapon even deadlier and more effective.

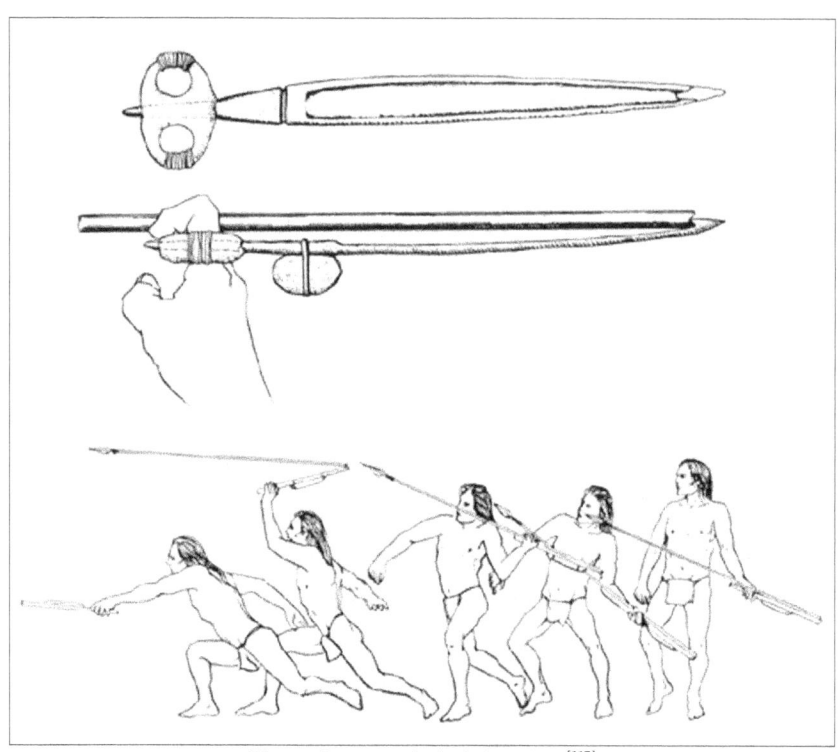
The ancient art of atlatl throwing.[117]

While the earliest archaeological evidence is around 25,000 years old, it is believed that the atlatl has been in use for over 40,000 years. About the time when paleoindians crossed into Beringia. The simplicity and effectiveness of this weapon had allowed these early humans to hunt Ice Age megafauna such as the Mammoth and other large game.

Eventually the development of the bow supplanted the atlatl as the weapon of choice in most of Mesoamerica. The bow was more compact and easier to carry, plus it was a much quieter weapon that allowed hunting prey easier.

Additionally when the megafauna animals ceased to

exist, the smaller mammals did not require the penetrative power delivered by the atlatl to bring them down.

It wasn't until the 16th Century, when the Spanish Conquistadors invaded that the Aztecs had re-adopted using the atlatl, Hand thrown spear and arrows fired by bows were not meeting their warfighting needs. They needed the atlatl with its increased power to penetrate the Spaniard's armor.

The Mesoamericans weren't able to compete against the Spaniard's cannon and firearms, but there were many a conquistador who were surprised to have an armor-piercing obsidian tipped dart pass completely through their steel breastplates. Piercing them through both front and back plates of the steel armor they had worn.

Atlatl throwing Aztec, Codex Becker.[118]

The Maya and other Mesoamerican people were able to fight the Spanish conquistadors. It required the Spaniards to use various Mesoamerican allies to help defeat the Maya. In a sense, the Spanish used the Maya to fight the Maya. Employing rival clans against each other.

References

Bookcover Photo: Copan Stela B. 12 February 2009.

1. Map of the Mayan Civilization cultural area by © Sémhur / Wikimedea Commons / CC-BY-SA-3.0 2. Martin & Grube 2000, p. 102. Sharer & Traxler 2006, p. 357.
2. Martin & Grube 2000, p. 102. Sharer & Traxler 2006, p. 357.
3. Sharer, Robert with Traxler, Loa. The Ancient Maya. p. 263.
4. Ortiz, P. & M. Del C. Rodriguez. 1999. Olmec ritual behavior at El Manati: a sacred space, in D.C. Grove & R.A. Joyce (ed.) Social Patterns in Pre-Classic Mesoamerica: 225-54. Washington (D.C.): Dumbarton Oaks.
5. Ortiz, P. & M. Del C. Rodriguez. 2000. The Sacred Hill of El Manati: A Preliminary Discussion of the Site's Ritual Paraphernalia, in J.E. Clark & M.E. Pye (ed.) Olmec Art and Archaeology in Mesoamerica (Studies in the History of Art 58): 75-93. Washington (D.C.): Center for Advanced Study in the Visual Arts, National Gallery of Art.
6. Love, M., D. Castillo, R. Ugarte, B. Damiata, & J. Steinberg. 2005. Investigaciones arqueologicas en el monticulo 1 de La Blanca, Costa Sur de Guatemala, in J.P. Laporte, B. Arroyo & H.E. Mejia (ed.) XVIII Simposio de Investigaciones Arqueologicas en Guatemala: 959-69. Guatemala City, Guatemala: Ministerio de Cultura y Deportes, Instituto de Antropologia e Historia, Asociacion Tikal, Foundation for the Advancement of Mesoamerican Studies, Inc.
7. Cyphers, A. 1993. Women, rituals, and social dynamics at ancient Chalcatzingo. Latin American Antiquity 4: 209-24.
8. Marcus, J. 1998. Women's Ritual in Formative Oaxaca: Figurine-making, Divination, Death, and the Ancestors. Memoirs 33. Ann Arbor:University of Michigan Museum of Anthropology.

9. Joyce, R.A. 2003. Making something of herself: embodiment in life and death at Playa de los Muertos, Honduras. Cambridge Archaeological Journal 13: 248-61.
10. Marcus, J. 1999. Men's and women's ritual in Formative Oaxaca, in D.C. Grove & R.A. Joyce (ed.) Social Patterns in Pre-Classic Mesoamerica: 67-96. Washington (D.C.): Dumbarton Oaks.
11. GROVE, D.C. & S.D. GILLESPIE. 2002. Middle Formative domestic ritual at Chalcatzingo, Morelos, in E Plunker (ed.) Domestic Ritual in Ancient Mesoamerica. (Cotsen Institue of Archeology Monograph 46): 11-19. Los Angeles: Cotsen Institute of Archaeology at UCLA
12. Acemoglu, Robinson, Daron, James A. (2012). Why Nations Fail. p. 143 ISBN 978-0-397-71921-8
13. Mayan Stela, Copan, Honduras
14. Mayan Figurines, 600-900AD made in Jaina, Maya Area, Campeche, Mexico. photo: Bruce M. White courtesy Princeton University Art Museum.
15. The Mayan Long Count Calendar. Photo credit: Hannah Gleghorn.
16. Mayan Calendar Diagram by Centro de Estudios del Mundo Maya.
17. Tzolkin Day Signs and Names Diagram by Centro de Estudios del Mundo Maya.
18. The Story of Writing: Alphabets, Hieroglyphs & Pictograms by Andrew Robinson Credit: Photo by Columbia Pictures.
19. Liz Sonneborn (January 2007). Chronology of the American Indian History. Infobase Publishing. p. 3. Retrieved 29 November 2011.
20. Jennifer Viegas (November 2009) "First Americans Endured 20,000-Year Layover." Retrieved 2009-11-18. Page 2.
21. "Method and Theory in American Archaeology". Gordon Willey and Philip Phillips. University of Chicago. 1958. Retrieved 2009-11-20.
22. "Learn about Y-DNA Haplogroup Q" (Verbal tutorial possible). Wendy Tymchuk - Senior Technical Editor. Genebase Systems. 2008. Retrieved 2009-11-21.
23. Paleo-Indians hunting a glytodont. Heinrich Harder (1858–1935), c.1920.
24. Jacobs, James Q. (2001). "The Paleoamericans: Issues and Evidence relating to the Peopling of the New World". Retrieved 2006-07-24.
25. Jacobs, James Q. (2002). "Paleoamerican origins: A Review of Hypotheses and Evidence Relating to the Origins of the First Americans". Retrieved 2006-07-24.
26. Obsidian Projectile Point. R. Villalobos, Museo de Arquelogia de Guatemala, Puerta Parada, 9500 BC.
27. "Blame North America Megafauna Extinction On Climate Change, Not

Human Ancestors". ScienceDaily. 2001.
28. Fiedel, Stuart J (1992). Prehistory of the Americas. Cambridge University Press.
29. Stuart B. Schwartz, Frank Salomon (1999-12-28). The Cambridge History of the Native Peoples of the Americas. Cambridge University Press.
30. Pielou, E.C. (1991). After the Ice Age : The Return of Life to Glaciated North America. University Of Chicago Press.
31. Atlatl weights and carved stone gorgets from Poverty Point. 2009-03-02 Heironymous Rowe CC-BY-SA-3.0; Released under GNU license.
32. Wm. Jack Hranicky; Wm Jack Hranicky Rpa (17 June 2010). North American Projectile Points - Revised. AuthorHouse. p. 135.
33. Vance T. Holliday (1997). Paleoindian geoarchaeology of the southern High Plains. University of Texas Press. p. 15.
34. The First Americans: In Pursuit of Archaeology's Greatest Mystery.. New York: Random House,. 2002. p. 14.
35. Wolfgang H. Berger; Elizabeth Noble Shor (25 April 2009).Ocean: reflections on a century of exploration. University of California Press. p. 397.
36. McHugh, Tom; Hobson, Victoria (1979). The Time of the Buffalo. University Of Nebraska Press.
37. Defrance, S. D.; Keefer, D. K.; Richardson, J. B.; Alvarez, A. n. U. (2010). "Late Paleo-Indian Coastal Foragers: Specialized Extractive". Susan D. deFrance, David K. Keefer, James B. Richardson and Adan Umire Alvarez (Society for American Archaeology) 12 (4): 413–426.
38. "Alberta History pre 1800". Jasper Alberta. 2009.
39. Bradley, B. and Stanford, D. "The North Atlantic ice-edge corridor: a possible Palaeolithic route to the New World." World Archaeology 34, 2004.
40. Lauber, Patricia. Who Came First? New Clues to Prehistoric Americans. Washington, D.C.: National Geographic Society, 2003.
41. "National Parks Service Southeastern Archaeological Center: The Paleoindian Period."
42. "Science News Online: Early New World Settlers Rise in East" Science News. 2000.
43. . National Historic Landmark summary listing. National Park Service.
44. "Monte Verde Archaeological Site - UNESCO World Heritage Centre".
45. "CNN.com: Man in Americas Earlier Than Thought". 2004-11-18.
46. Ignacio Villarreal (2010-08-25). "Mexican Archaeologists Extract 10,000 Year-Old Skeleton from Flooded Cave in Quintana Roo".
47. "Skull in Underwater Cave May Be Earliest Trace of First Americans -

NatGeo News Watch". 2011-02-18.
48. "Does skull prove that the first Americans came from Europe?". The University of Texas at Austin - Web Central
49. Jordan, David K (2009). "Prehistoric Beringia". University of California-San Diego.
50. Bernal Díaz's Verdadera Historia de la Conquista de Nueva España (The Conquest of New Spain), pp.59–66.
51. The shoals are named as Los Alacranes ("the scorpions") by Bernal Díaz and Cervantes de Salazar, with Cervantes also calling them Las Viboras ("the vipers"). See Ch. XXII of Crónica de la Nueva España, and also The Valdivia Shipwreck (1511), which follows Cervantes
52. The landing place is around the "Rio Hondo" or possibly Cozumel or a little further to the south. See The Valdivia Shipwreck (1511) (1999).
53. Bernal Díaz uses the term Cacique, a word deriving from Caribbean languages such as Taíno and used by the Spanish generally for tribal chieftains; he also gives the word Calachiones as the local title. See The Conquest of New Spain, p.65.
54. Clendinnen, Inga; Ambivalent Conquests: Maya and Spaniard in Yucatán, 1517-1570. (pgs 11-12).
55. The numbers for Grijalva's expedition are as given by Bernal Díaz, who participated in the voyage. See Díaz del Castillo (1963, p.27).
56. Guerrero is reported by Bernal Díaz to have responded, "Brother Aguilar, I am married and have three children, and they look on me as a Cacique here, and a captain in time of war....But my face is tattooed and my ears are pierced. What would the Spaniards say if they saw me like this? And look how handsome these children of mine are!" (p.60). However, other 16th-century sources say that Aguilar did not actually talk to Guerrero in person, but merely sent him a message (Gómara's version) or was unable to communicate with him at all (Cortés, de Landa), since if Guerrero was indeed near Chetumal that was some 400km from Cozumel. The quote attributed to Guerrero may well be a dramatic invention of Díaz. See discussion in Romero (1992, pp.7–10).
57. Later in the voyage a young woman, La Malinche, would be given to Cortés as a slave by the Chontal Maya inhabitants of the Tabasco coast. La Malinche spoke Nahuatl, the language of the Aztecs and a regional lingua franca, as well as Chontal Maya, which was also understood by Aguilar. Cortés used those two to communicate with the central Mexican peoples and the Aztec court. The Conquest of New Spain, pp.85–87.
58. Clendinnen, Inga; Ambivalent Conquests: Maya and Spaniard in Yucatan, (pg 23) 1517-1570.

59. Jones, Grant D. (1998). The Conquest of the Last Maya Kingdom. Stanford, California, USA: Stanford University Press
60. Feldman, Lawrence H. (2000). Lost Shores, Forgotten Peoples: Spanish Explorations of the South East Maya Lowlands. Durham, North Carolina, US: Duke University Press.
61. Lovell, W. George (2005). Conquest and Survival in Colonial Guatemala: A Historical Geography of the Cuchumatán Highlands, 1500–1821 (3rd ed.). Montreal, Canada: McGill-Queen's University Press.
62. Hardoy, Jorge E. (July 1991). "Antiguas y Nuevas Capitales Nacionales de América Latina". Revista EURE (Revista Latinoamericana de Estudios Urbanos Regionales) (Santiago, Chile: Universidad Católica de Chile) XVII (52/53): 7–26.
63. Schwartz, Norman B. (1990). Forest Society: A Social History of Petén, Guatemala. Ethnohistory. Philadelphia, Pennsylvania, USA: University of Pennsylvania Press
64. Jones, Grant D. (2009). "The Kowoj in Ethnohistorical Perspective". In Prudence M. Rice and Don S. Rice (eds.). The Kowoj: identity, migration, and geopolitics in late postclassic Petén, Guatemala. Boulder, Colorado, US: The University Press Colorado. pp. 55–69.
65. Rice, Prudence M. and Don S. Rice (2009). "Introduction to the Kowoj and their Petén Neighbors". In Prudence M. Rice and Don S. Rice (eds.). The Kowoj: identity, migration, and geopolitics in late postclassic Petén, Guatemala. Boulder, Colorado, US: The University Press Colorado.
66. The 'macuahuitl': model displayed as part of the British Museum Moctezuma exhibition, London (bottom); artist's impression by Felipe Dávalos (top). Photos by Ian Mursell/Mexicolore.
67. Maya ruler, warrior, peasant levy Based on the Bonampak murals, a gold disc found on the Sacred Cenote in Chicen Itza and terracotta figurines from the island of Jaina. Source: Osprey Military Men-At-Arms series 101 "The Conquistadores" by Terence Wise. Illustrator: Angus McBride.
68. Means, Philip Ainsworth (1917). History of the Spanish Conquest of Yucatan and of the Itzas. Papers of the Peabody Museum of American Archaeology and Ethnology, Harvard University. VII. Cambridge, Massachussetts, USA: Peabody Museum of Archaeology and Ethnology.
69. Feldman, Lawrence H. (2000). Lost Shores, Forgotten Peoples: Spanish Explorations of the South East Maya Lowlands. Durham, North Carolina, US: Duke University Press.

70. Rice, Prudence M. (2009a). "The Archaeology of the Kowoj: Settlement and Architecture at Zacpetén". In Prudence M. Rice and Don S. Rice (eds.). The Kowoj: identity, migration, and geopolitics in late postclassic Petén, Guatemala. Boulder, Colorado, US: University Press of Colorado. pp. 81–83
71. Pugh, Timothy W. (2009). "Residential and Domestic Contexts at Zacpetén". In Prudence M. Rice and Don S. Rice (eds.). The Kowoj: identity, migration, and geopolitics in late postclassic Petén, Guatemala. Boulder, Colorado, US: University Press of Colorado. pp. 141–191.
72. Drawing accompanying text in Book XII of the 16th-century Florentine Codex (compiled 1540–1585), showing Nahuas of conquest-era central Mexico suffering from smallpox.
73. Chichen Itza at Spring Equinox photo by Shawn Christie. Chichen Itza at Spring Equinox during the equinox the sun casts its rays on the pyramid, forming seven isosceles triangles that resemble the body of a serpent 37 yards long slithering downwards until it joins the huge serpent's head carved in stone at the bottom of the stairway. It is said this snake is trying to make it to the well of sacrifice which is in the same direction. This photo was taken that day after the actual spring equinox. The day prior was cloudy and no serpent was seen. This photo was taken on March 22, 2010 in Chichén-Itzá, Yucatan, MX, using a Nikon D300.
74. Sculpture in the Temple of the Warriors, Chichén Itzá Yucatán, Mexico. Photo by Jeremy Woodhouse.
75. The Pyramid of Kukulcan seen from the Temple of the Warriors at Chichen-Itza.
76. Kaplan, Jonathan (2011) Conclusion: The Southern Maya Region and the Problem of Unities. In The Southern Maya in the Late Preclassic: The Rise and Fall of an Early Mesoamerican Civilization. Michael W. Love and Jonathan Kaplan, eds.; 490-532. University Press of Colorado, Boulder.
77. Kaplan, Jonathan (2008) Hydraulics, Cacao, and Complex Developments at Preclassic Chocolá, Guatemala: Evidence and Implications. Latin American Antiquity 19(4):399-413.
78. Herr, Sarah H. "The Latest Research on the Earliest Farmers." Archaeology Southwest. Vol. 23, No. 1, Winter 2009, p. 1
79. 1491: New Revelations of the Americas Before Columbus by Charles C. Mann, 2005.
80. Portion of the hieroglyphic Stairway with Maya glyphs at El Palmar. The fragmented block represents an emblem glyph of Kaan (Snake)

dynasty at Calakmul, one of the most powerful Ancient Maya dynasties. Photo by Kenichiro Tsukamoto.
81. The Meaning of Words: New Evidence of Ancient Maya History. by Fabio Esteban Amador of National Geographic Waitt Grants Program onApril 25, 2011.
82. Calakmul largest pyramid, referred to as Structure 2. Photo credit: Pete Fordham.
83. One of Three Scribes in Mural from Maya House 10K-2 at Xultun Photo by Tyrone Turner © 2012 National Geographic.
84. Maya warrior from set of History Channel's "Warriors: Maya Armegadon." Photo by Tom Mills, 2009.
85. Robert H. Fuson, ed., The Log of Christopher Columbus, Tab Books, 1992, International Marine Publishing.
86. Columbus (1991, p.87). Or "for with fifty men they can all be subjugated and made to do what is required of them." (Columbus & Toscanelli, 2010, p.41).
87. Bakewell, Peter. A History of Latin America. Blackwell Publishers, pp. 129–130.
88. The Doctrine of Discovery and the Christian Conquest of the World." By Nick Gier, Professor Emeritus, University of Idaho.
89. Collection des Mémoires sur l'Amérique, Recueil des Pièces sur le Mexique trad., par Ternaux-Compans, p. 307.
90. Salisbury, Stephen (2012-05-12). The Mayas, the Sources of Their History Dr. Le Plongeon in Yucatan, His Account of Discoveries.
91. Relation des choses de Yucatan. By Diego de Landa, Paris, 1864, pp. 44, 316.
92. Salisbury, Stephen (2012-05-12). The Mayas, the Sources of Their History Dr. Le Plongeon in Yucatan, His Account of Discoveries.
93. Relacion de las Cosas de Yucatan, de Diego de Landa. By L. Abbé Brasseur de Bourbourg. Paris, 1864, page 347.
94. Petén. Clay. height 14.8 cm Seated figure with removable helmet (Kohaw).
95. Aveni, Anthony F., Empires of Time, Tauris Parke Paperbacks, 2000.
96. Ruggles, Clive L.N., Ancient Astronomy, ABC-CLIO, 2005.
97. Anzovin, Steven et al., Famous First Facts International Edition, H. W. Wilson Company (2000).
98. The Dresden Codex, pp. 47, 48, 50, 51, 52, first redrawing by Humboldt in 1810. Alexander von Humboldt: Vues des Cordillères et Monuments des Peuples Indigènes de l'Amérique. Paris, 1810, p. 416, Plate 45.
99. Teresi, Dick, Lost Discoveries: The Ancient Roots of Modern Science— from the Babylonians to the Maya, Simon and Schuster, 2002.

100. Nikolai Grube: Der Dresdner Maya-Kalender: Der vollständige Codex. Verlag Herder, Freiburg, 2012.
101. Sharer, Robert J.; with Loa P. Traxler (2006). The Ancient Maya (6th, fully revised ed.). Stanford, California: Stanford University Press.
102. Noguez, Xavier; Manuel Hermann Lejarazu ;Merideth Paxton and Henrique Vela (August 2009). "Códices Mayas [Maya codices]". Arqueología Mexicana: Códices prehispánicos y coloniales tempranos – Catálogo (Editorial Raíces) Special Edition (31): 10–23.
103. Ciudad Ruiz, Andrés; and Alfonso Lacadena (1999). J.P. Laporte and H.L. Escobedo. ed. "El Códice Tro-Cortesiano de Madrid en el contexto de la tradición escrita Maya [The Tro-Cortesianus Codex of Madrid in the context of the Maya writing tradition]" . Simposio de Investigaciones Arqueológicas en Guatemala, 1998 (Guatemala City, Guatemala: Museo Nacional de Arqueología y Etnología): 876–888.
104. Madrid Codex (replica) in the Museum of the Americas, Madrid. Late Postclassic Maya book. Simon Burchell 14 April 2012.
105. The Codex Perez; An Ancient Mayan Hieroglyphic Book, A photographic facsimile reproduced from the original in the Bibliothèque Nationale, Paris, by Theodore A. Willard. Glendale, California: The Arthur H. Clark Company, 1933.
106. Bruce Love "The Paris Codex." Austin: University of Texas Press. 1994.
107. Paris Codex, leaves 21-22 from Compendio Xcaret.
108. The pyramid in the Mayan city of Chichen Itza. Photograph: Steve Allen/Getty Images.
109. Early Civilizations in the Americas: Almanac. (2005). Gale Cengage.
110. Gibbard, P. and van Kolfschoten, T. (2004) "The Pleistocene and Holocene Epochs" Chapter 22. In Gradstein, F. M., Ogg, James G., and Smith, A. Gilbert (eds.), A Geologic Time Scale 2004 Cambridge University Press, Cambridge.
111. Field Museum (2008, February 28). Centuries-old Maya Blue Mystery Finally Solved. ScienceDaily.
112. A mural depicting ancient Maya heart extraction at Chichén Itzá in Mexico Bristol Museum. Photo Norman Hammond.
113. Aoyama, Kazuo (2005). "Classic Maya Warfare and Weapons spear, dart, and arrow points of Aguateca and Copan". Ancient Mesoamerica (Cambridge University Press) 16 (2): 291–304.
114. Barrett, Jason W.; and Andrew K. Scherer (2005). "Stones Bones and Crowded Plazas Evidence for Terminal Classic Maya warfare at Colha, Belize". Ancient Mesoamerica (Cambridge University Press) 16 (1): 101–18.
115. Vidal Lorenzo, Cristina; Juan Antonio Valdés and Gaspar Muñoz

Cosme (2007). "El Clásico Terminal y el abandono de los palacios de La Blanca, Petén." XX Simposio de Investigaciones Arqueológicas en Guatemala, 2006 (edited by J.P. Laporte, B. Arroyo and H. Mejía). Museo Nacional de Arqueología y Etnología, Guatemala. pp. 561–576.

116. Vidal Lorenzo, Cristina; and Gaspar Muñoz Cosme (Undated). "Guatemala: La ciudad Maya de La Blanca". Madrid, Spain: Museo Nacional Centro de Arte Reina Sofía. pp. 45–50.
117. The ancient art of atlatl throwing by Wikipedia.
118. Atlatl throwing, Codex Becker, fol. 10. Graz, Austria, 1961.
119. Sanders, William and David Webster (1988) The Mesoamerican Urban Tradition. American Anthropologist 90(3): 521-546.
120. Howler monkey statue, temple 11, World Heritage Site of Copan (13 May 2009). Adalberto Hernandez Vega from Copan Ruinas, Honduras.
121. The Maize God as scribe. Francis Robicsek: The Maya Book of the Dead. The Ceramic Codex, University of Virginia Art Museum (1981).
122. Foster, Lynn V. (2001) Handbook to Life in the Ancient Maya World. New York: Facts on File, Inc..
123. Bunson, Margaret R., and Stephen M. Bunson. (1996) Warfare, Maya. Encyclopedia of Ancient Mesoamerica. New York: Facts On File, Inc., 1996.
124. Barrett, Jason and Andrew Scherer. (2005) Stones, Bones, and Crowded Plazas: Evidence for Terminal Classic Maya Warfare at Colha, Belize. Ancient Mesoamerica 16(1): 101-118.
125. S.W. Miles, The Sixteenth-Century Pokom-Maya. The American Philosophical Society, Philadelphia 1957. pg 749, quoting Fuentes y Guzmán and Las Casas.
126. Evon Z. Vogt, Tortillas for the Gods. A Symbolic Analysis of Zinacanteco Rituals. Harvard University Press, Cambridge 1976.
127. Barbara Tedlock, Time and the Highland Maya. University of New Mexico Pres, Albuquerque 1992.
128. Ralph L. Roys, The Book of Chilam Balam of Chumayel. University of Oklahoma Press, Norman 1967.
129. Bruce Love, 'Yucatec Sacred Breads Through Time'. In William F. Hanks and Don Rice, Word and Image in Maya Culture. Salt Lake City: University of Utah Press 1989.
130. Thompson, J. Eric S. (1970). Maya History and Religion. Civilization of the American Indian Series, No. 99. Norman: University of Oklahoma Press.
131. Alfred M. Tozzer, Landa's Relación de las cosas de Yucatán. A Translation. Peabody Museum, Cambridge MA 1941.
132. Alfred M. Tozzer, A Comparative Study of the Mayas and the

Lacandones. Archaeological Institute of America. The Macmillan Company, New York 1907.
133. Accession: see Piedras Negras stela 11; illness and burial: Las Casas, in Miles 1957: 750, 773; drought: Landa, in Tozzer 1941: 54, 180-181.
134. David Joralemon, 'Ritual Blood Sacrifice Among the Ancient Maya: Part I', in Primera Mesa Redonda de Palenque Part II, pp. 59–75. The Robert Louis Stevenson School, Pre-Columbian Art Research, Pebble Beach 1974.
135. Joyce, Rosemary; Richard Edging; Karl Lorenz and Susan Gillespie (1991). "Olmec Bloodletting: An Iconographic Study". In V M Fields. Sixth Palenque Round Table 1986. Norman, Oklahoma, USA.: University of Oklahoma Press.
136. Bancroft, Hubert Howe (1882). The Native Races, Volume 2, Civilized Nations.
137. Joralemon, D. (1974). "Ritual Blood-Sacrifice among the Ancient Maya: Part I". In Merle Green Robertson (ed.). Primera Mesa Redonda de Palenque. Pebble Beach, California, USA: Robert Louis Stevenson School, Pre-Columbian Art Research. pp. 59–76.
138. De Landa, Diego (1937). Yucatan Before and After the Conquest: An English translation by William Gates of Relation des choses de Yucatan de Diego de Landa.
139. Montero Lopez, Coral (July 2009). "Sacrifice and feasting among the classic Maya elite, and the importance of the white-tailed deer: is there a regional pattern?". Journal of Historical and European Studies (Bundoora, Victoria, Australia: School of Historical and European Studies, La Trobe University) 2: 53–68.
140. Marcus, Joyce (October 1978). "Archaeology and Religion: A Comparison of the Zapotec and Maya". World Archaeology (Abingdon, UK.: Routledge Journals) 10 (2): 172–191.
141. Tiesler, Vera; Andrea Cucina (December 2006). "Procedures in Human Heart Extraction and Ritual Meaning: A Taphonomic Assessment of Anthropogenic Marks in Classic Maya Skeletons". Latin American Antiquity 17 (4): 493–510.
142. de Anda Alanís, Guillermo (2007). "Sacrifice and Ritual Body Mutilation in Postclassical Maya Society: Taphonomy of the Human Remains from Chichén Itzá's Cenote Sagrado". In Vera Tiesler and Andrea Cucina (eds.). New Perspectives on Human Sacrifice and Ritual Body Treatments in Ancient Maya Society. Interdisciplinary Contributions to Archaeology. Michael Jochim (series ed.). New York, USA.: Springer Verlag. pp. 190–208.
143. Baudez, Claude F.; and Peter Matthews (1978 or 1979). "Capture and

sacrifice at Palenque". In Merle Greene Robertson and Donnan Call Jeffers. Tercera Mesa Redonda de Palenque. IV.
144. Stuart, David (2003). "La ideología del sacrificio entre los mayas". Arqueología mexicana (Mexico City.: Editorial Raíces) XI (63): 24–29.
145. Pendergast, David M. (1988). "Lamanai Stela 9: The Archaeological Context". Research Reports on Ancient Maya Writings 20. Washington DC, USA.: Centre for Maya Research.
146. Marí, Carlos (27 December 2005). "Evidencian sacrificios humanos en Comalcaco: Hallan entierro de menores mayas". Reforma.
147. Eppich, Keith (2009). "Feast and Sacrifice at El Perú-Waka': The N14-2 Deposit as Dedication". The PARI Journal X (2).
148. Lee, J.C. (1996). The Amphibians and Reptiles of the Yucatan Peninsula. New York, USA.: Cornell University.
149. Reilly, F.Kent (1991). "Olmec iconographic influences on symbols of Maya rulership". Sixth Palenque Round Table 1986. Norman, Oklahoma, USA.: University of Oklahoma Press.
150. Berryman, Carrie Anne. (2007) "Captive Sacrifice and Trophy Taking Among the Ancient Maya" in The Taking and Displaying of Human Body Parts By Amerindians, edited by Richard J Chacon & David H Dye, pp. 377-399. Chapter 13. Springer Science + Business Media, New York.
151. McAnany, A. Patricia (1998). "Ancestors and the Classic Maya Built Environme."
152. O'Mansky, Matt & Arthur A Demarest. (2007) "Status Rivalry and Warfare in the Development and Collapse of Classic Maya Civilization" in Latin American Indigenous Warfare and Ritual Violence, edited by Richard J Chacon & Ruben G Mendoza, pp. 11-34. Chapter 1. The University of Arizona Press, Tucson.
153. Spence, W. Michael; Christine D. White, Fred J. Longstaffe, and Kimberly R. Law (2004). Human Trophies Worn by the Sacrificial Soldiers from the Feathered Serpent Pyramid, Teotihuacan. New York: Cambridge University Press.
154. Casas. "Apologética Historia Sumaria." 1967: 504-505
155. López Austin, Alfredo; and Leonardo López Luján (1999). Mito y realidad de Zuyuá: Serpiente emplumada y las transformaciones mesoamericanas del clásico al posclásico. Mexico: COLMEX & FCE. ISBN 968-16-5889-2.
156. Teotihuacan - Temple of the Feathered Serpent. 14 April 2008. Wikimedia Commons.
157. Allen J. Christenson, Art and Sociey in a Highland Maya Community: The Altarpiece of Santiago Atitlán. Austin: University of Texas Press.

2001.
158. Rafael Girard, Los Chortis ante el problema maya. Guatemala: Editorial Cultura. 1949.
159. Barbara Tedlock, Time and the Highland Maya. University of New Mexico Pres, Albuquerque 1992.
160. David Stuart, The Order of Days. Harmony Books, New York 2011.
161. Orellana, Sandra L. (Spring 1981). "Idols and Idolatry in Highland Guatemala". Ethnohistory (Duke University Press) 28 (2): 157–177.
162. David Stuart, The Inscriptions from Temple XIX at Palenque. San Francisco: The Pre-Columbian Art Research Institute 2005.
163. Michael D. Coe, 'A Model of Ancient Maya Community Structure in the Maya Lowlands', Southwestern Journal of Anthropology 21 (1965).
164. Linda A. Brown, 'Planting the Bones: Hunting Ceremonialism at Contemporary and Nineteenth-Century Shrines in the Guatemalan Highlands', Latin American Antiquity 16(2): 131-146 (2005).
165. Victor Montejo, El Kanil, Man of Lightning. Signal Books, Carrboro N.C. 1984.
166. Francisco de Fuentes y Guzmán, Recordación Florida. 2 vols. Madrid: Atlas. 1969.
167. Takeshi Inomata, 'Plazas, Performers, and Spectators'. Current Anthropology 47 (5), 2006.
168. Martin, Simon, and Nikolai Grube, Chronicle of Maya Kings and Queens. Thames&Hudson 2000.
169. Nikolai Grube and Werner Nahm, 'A Census of Xibalba', in Maya Vase Books Vol. 4, New York 1994. Kerr Associates.
170. J.E.S. Thompson, Maya Hieroglyphic Writing. University of Oklahoma Press, Norman 1960. pg 71, quoting Nuñez de la Vega.
171. Robert S. Carlson, and Martin Prechtel, 'The Flowering of the Dead: An Interpretation of Highland Maya Culture'. Man 26-1 (1991): 22-42.
172. Calixta Guiteras Holmes, Perils of the Soul. The World View of a Tzotzil Indian. New York: The Free Press of Glencoe. 1961.
173. Kerry Hull, 'The Grand Ch'orti' Epic: The Story of the Kumix Angel'. Acta Mesoamericana 20 (2009): 131-140.
174. The Hero Twins shooting a perched bird demon with a blowgun. Izapa Stela 25. Drawing of Izapa Stela 25 taken from Japanese Wikipedia. 20 February 2006.
175. Gabrielle Vail, 'Pre-Hispanic Maya Religion. Conceptions of divinity in the Postclassic Maya codices'. Ancient Mesoamerica 11(2000): 123-147.
176. Scholes, France V., and Ralph L. Roys, The Maya Chontal Indians of Acalan-Tixchel. University of Oklahoma Press, Norman 1968.
177. Sarah C. Blaffer, The Black-man of Zinacantan. University of Texas

Press, Austin 1972.
178. Boremanse, Didier, Contes et mythologie des indiens lacandons. Paris: L'Harmattan. 1986. (Also in Spanish: Cuentos y mitología de los lacandones. Tradición oral maya. Editorial: Academia de Geografia e Historia de Guatemala.).
179. Lauren Landry (December 11th, 2012). "Boston University Professor Reminds Us: The Mayan Calendar Doesn't Say the World Will End". BostInno.
180. Bierhorst, John (ed.), The Monkey's Haircut and Other Stories Told by the Maya. New York: William Morrow 1986.
181. Nicholson, Irene, Mexican and Central American Mythology. London: Paul Hamlyn. 1967.
182. Danien, Elin C., Maya Folktales from the Alta Verapaz. University of Pennsylvania, Museum of Archaeology and Anthropology, Philadelphia 2004.
183. Bierhorst,John, The Mythology of Mexico and Central America. Oxford U.P. 2002.
184. Roys, Ralph L. (translator), The Book of Chilam Balam of Chumayel. Norman: University of Oklahoma Press, 1967 [1933].
185. Copy of the Book of Chilam Balam of Ixil in the National Museum of Anthropology, Mexico City. 8 July 2008.
186. Paxton, Merideth (2001). 'Books of Chilam Balam', in: Oxford Encyclopedia of Mesoamerican Cultures Vol. 1. Oxford: Oxford University Press.
187. Knowlton, Timothy (2010). Maya Creation Myths: Words and Worlds of the Chilam Balam. Boulder: University Press of Colorado.
188. Christenson, Allen J. (trans.), ed. Popol Vuh: Literal Poetic Version: Translation and Transcription. Norman: University of Oklahoma Press. 2004.
189. Goetz, Delia, and Morley, Sylvanus Griswold, ed. Popol Vuh: The Sacred Book of the Ancient Quiché Maya By Adrián Recinos (1st ed.). Norman: University of Oklahoma Press. 1950.
190. The oldest written account of Popol Vuh. 1701 AD by Francisco Ximénez. Primera página del manuscrito del Popol Vuh, guardado en la Biblioteca de Newberry, Chicago, Colección Ayer. Wikimedia Commons. 17 April 2012.
191. Roys, Ralph L., Ritual of the Bacabs, University of Oklahoma Press. 1965.
192. Thompson, J. Eric S., Maya History and Religion, University of Oklahoma Press. 1970.
193. Table showing first 20 Maya numbers and their Arabic equivalents.

Centro de Estudios del Mundo Maya. Yucatan, Mexico. Maya World Studies Center.
194. Freidel, David; and Linda Schele and Joy Parker (1993). Maya Cosmos: Three thousand years on the shaman's path. New York: William Morrow. ISBN [[Special:BookSources/0-88810-081-5|0-88810-081-5]]. OCLC 27430287.
195. Thompson, J. Eric S. (1929). "Maya Chronology: Glyph G of the Lunar Series". American Anthropologist, New Series 31 (2): pp.223–231. doi:10.1525/aa.1929.31.2.02a00010. ISSN 0002-7294. OCLC 51205515.
196. Thompson, J. Eric S. (1971). Maya Hieroglyphic Writing, an Introduction. 3rd edition. Norman.
197. "Clarifications: The Correlation Debate." Excerpt from Tzolkin: Visionary Perspectives and Calendar Studies (Borderlands Science and Research Foundation, 1994, pages 31-36):
198. John Major Jenkins. "Tzolkin: Visionary Perspectives and Calendar Studies." Borderland Sciences Research Foundation; First Printing edition (1994). ISBN-10: 0945685165.
199. "Maya." Dictionary.com Unabridged. Random House, Inc. 19 Jan. 2013.
200. Picture of Temple I in Tikal, Guatemala, taken by Bruno Girin. (2005).
201. Sharer, Robert J.; with Loa P. Traxler (2006). The Ancient Maya (6th (fully revised) ed.). Stanford, CA: Stanford University Press. ISBN 0-8047-4817-9. OCLC 57577446.
202. The Mayan ruins of Copan Ruinas located near Copan, Honduras. Photograph by Kyle Hammons. July 14, 2009.
203. Hypothesized map of human migration based on mitochondrial DNA. Illustration by Mauricio Lucioni. 8 April 2010.
204. Paleoindian Point Types. "The Taking Of South America In Atlantean Times." frontiers-of-anthropology.blogspot.com. February 10, 2112.
205. John F. Hoffecker, Scott A. Elias. "Human Ecology of Beringia." June 2007. ISBN: 978-0-231-13060-8.
206. Bering Land Bridge. Survey of Meteorology. Thomson Higher Education. 2007.
207. Map: "The Bering Strait Land Bridge and the Migration of Early Indians" By Jose Arredondo, University of California Los Angeles.
208. Jennifer Viegas. "First Americans Endured 20,000-Year Layover." Discovery News. Feb. 13, 2008.
209. Kitchen A, Miyamoto MM, Mulligan CJ (2008) A Three-Stage Colonization Model for the Peopling of the Americas. PLoS ONE 3(2): e1596. doi:10.1371/journal.pone.0001596.
210. Mulligan CJ, Kitchen A, Miyamoto MM (2008) Updated Three-Stage

Model for the Peopling of the Americas. PLoS ONE 3(9): e3199. doi:10.1371/journal.pone.0003199.
211. Maps depicting each phase of our three-step colonization model for the peopling of the Americas. From figure 4. Kitchen A, Miyamoto MM, Mulligan CJ (2008) A Three-Stage Colonization Model for the Peopling of the Americas. PLoS ONE 3(2): e1596. doi:10.1371/journal.pone.0001596.
212. Inga Clendinnen. "Ambivalent Conquests: Maya and Spaniard in Yucatan, 1517-1570." Cambridge University Press. Apr 28, 2003.
213. Lidded effigy container in the form of a diving god ca. A.D. 1500. Late Postclassic Maya. Princeton University Art Museum.
214. Paleo-Indians butchering a bison at the end of the Ice Age with woolly mammoths looking on. Painting on exhibit at the Pembina State Museum, courtesy of the State Historical Society of North Dakota.
215. E.C. Pielou, After the Ice Age: The Return of Life to Glaciated North America (Chicago: University of Chicago Press) 1991:19 and note.
216. Gordon R. Willey and Philip Phillips (1957). Method and Theory in American Archaeology. University of Chicago Press. ISBN 978-0-226-89888-9.
217. "Archaic Period, Southeast Archaeological Center". Archived from the original on 5 December 2004.
218. Joe W. Saunders, Rolfe D. Mandel, Roger T. Saucier, E. Thurman Allen, C. T. Hallmark, Jay K. Johnson, Edwin H. Jackson, Charles M. Allen, Gary L. Stringer, Douglas S. Frink, James K. Feathers, Stephen Williams, Kristen J. Gremillion, Malcolm F. Vidrine, and Reca Jones, "A Mound Complex in Louisiana at 5400-5000 Years Before the Present", Science, 19 September 1997: Vol. 277 no. 5333, pp. 1796-1799.
219. Milanich, Jerald T. (1994). Archaeology of Precolumbian Florida. Gainesville, Florida: The University Press of Florida.
220. Michael Russo. "Archaic Shell Rings of the Southeast U.S." Southeast Archeological Center, National Park Service, Tallahassee. April 2006.
221. Archaic: 5500 to 500 B.C.- Overview. Crow Canyon Archaeological Center. 2011.
222. Time-Life Book Editors. (1993) The First Americans. Alexandria, Virginia: Time-Life Books. pp. 29, 30. ISBN 0-8094-9400-0.
223. Archaic camp scene by Martin Pate (Courtesy, Southeast Archeological Center, National Park Service).
224. Circa 5000 BC. Life-size mural by Greg Harlin.
225. Copan Stela B, dates to 731. One of the Great Kings: 18 Rabbits. Honduras. January 9, 2004.
226. An illustration showing Mayans playing the sacred ball game.

.theancientweb.org.
227. Maya logogram of calendric Tzolkin Day20:Ajaw. Image created by CJLL Wright.
228. Lockhart, James (2001). Nahuatl as Written: Lessons in Older Written Nahuatl, with Copious Examples and Texts. UCLA Latin American studies, vol. 88; Nahuatl studies series, no. 6. Stanford and Los Angeles: Stanford University Press and UCLA Latin American Center Publications. ISBN 0-8047-4282-0. OCLC 46858459.
229. Schroeder, Susan (2007). "The Annals of Chimalpahin". In James Lockhart, Lisa Sousa, and Stephanie Wood (eds.). Sources and Methods for the Study of Postconquest Mesoamerican Ethnohistory (Provisional version ed.). Eugene: University of Oregon Wired Humanities Project. Retrieved 2008-05-16.
230. Schroeder, Susan (1991). Chimalpahin and the Kingdoms of Chalco. Tucson: University of Arizona Press. ISBN 0-8165-1182-9. OCLC 21976206.
231. Nahuatl dictionary (1997). Wired humanities project.
232. Coe, Michael D. "The Maya scribe and his World." Grolier Club (1973). ISBN: 978-0813905686.
233. HM 626: Kneeling Warrior with Shield. 600-900 AD, Mexico. Palmer Collection.
234. The Ball Court at Copán, Honduras. by Tatiana Proskouriakoff. Peabody Museum of Archaeology and Ethnology, Harvard College.
235. Map of Settlement area of Ancient Maya. Nepenthes, 18 July 2006.
236. Map of North America showing the extent of Late Pleistocene glaciation. Modified after Pielou, 1991.
237. Walker, M., S. Johnsen, S.O. Rasmussen, T. Popp, J.-P. Steffensen, P. Gibbard, W. Hoek, J. Lowe, A. John, B. John, S. Björck, L.C. Cwynar, K. Hughen, K. Konrad, K. Peter, B. Kromer, T. Litt, D.J. Lowe, T. Nakagawa, R. Newnham, and J. Schwander (2008) Formal definition and dating of the GSSP (Global Stratotype Section and Point) for the base of the Holocene using the Greenland NGRIP ice core, and selected auxiliary records. Journal of Quaternary Science. 24(1):3–17.
238. Columbian mammoths were larger than mastodons. Both once roamed North America. (Velizar Simeonovski / The Field Museum, Chicago). Smithsonian magazine, April 2010.
239. San Lorenzo Monument 3 (also known as Colossal Head 3). Height: 178 cm. Museo de Antropología de Xalapa, Veracruz, Mexico. Photo by Maribel Ponce Ixba. 16 November 2006.
240. Burnett, R. L., Terry, R. E., Sweetwood, R. V., Webster, D., Murtha, T., & Silverstein, J.. Upland and Lowland Soil Resources of the Ancient Maya at Tikal, Guatemala. Soil Sci. Soc. Am. J.. 2012 76: 2083–2096.
241. Vernon L. Scarborough, Nicholas P. Dunning, Kenneth B. Tankersley,

Christopher Carr, Eric Weaver, Liwy Grazioso, Brian Lane, John G. Jones, Palma Buttles, Fred Valdez, and David L. Lentz. "Water and sustainable land use at the ancient tropical city of Tikal, Guatemala". PNAS 2012.
242. "Classic Period collapse of the Central Maya Lowlands: Insights about human-environment relationships for sustainability". B. L. Turner and J. A. Sabloff. Proceedings of the National Academy of Sciences (2012) 109: 13908.
243. These are veneer stones of the dam identified by the UC researchers. What was once thought to be a sluice is outlined in red and is now filled with slump-down debris [Photo and Research Credit: University of Cincinnati researchers]. 2012.
244. "Development and Disintegration of Maya Political Systems in Response to Climate Change". Douglas J. Kennett, Sebastian F. M. Breitenbach, Valorie V. Aquino, Yemane Asmerom, Jaime Awe, James U.L. Baldini, Patrick Bartlein, Brendan J. Culleton, Claire Ebert, Christopher Jazwa, Martha J. Macri, Norbert Marwan, Victor Polyak, Keith M. Prufer, Harriet E. Ridley, Harald Sodemann, Bruce Winterhalder, and Gerald H. Haug. Science 9 November 2012: 338 (6108), 788-791. [DOI:10.1126/science.1226299].
245. William L. Merrill, Robert J. Hard, Jonathan B. Mabry, Gayle J. Fritz, Karen R. Adams, John R. Roney, and A. C. MacWilliams . "The diffusion of maize to the southwestern United States and its impact". PNAS 2009.
246. A map of the southern-most area of Mesoamerica, showing important Formative Period sites. February 2008.
247. Illustration: Mirador Basin. "El Mirador, the Lost City of the Maya." Smithsonian magazine, May 2011.
248. Map of Preclassic Maya sites. Latin American Studies. Maya Maps. 2013.
249. Map of Maya Trade Routes. Latin American Studies. Maya Maps. 2013.
250. Map of New Spain in red, with territories claimed but not controlled in orange. Map of Viceroyalty of New Spain / Mapa del Virreinato de la Nueva España (siglo XVIII).
251. Georges Ifrah, "From One to Zero, a Universal History of Numbers", Penguin Books, 1987.
252. Hernan Garcia, Antonio Sierra, Gilberto Balam, Jeff Conant, and Hilberto Balam. "Wind in the Blood: Mayan Healing & Chinese Medicine." 1999.
253. G Ifrah, A universal history of numbers : From prehistory to the

invention of the computer (London, 1998).
254. J B Lambert, B Ownbey-McLaughlin, and C D McLaughlin, Maya arithmetic, Amer. Sci. 68 (3) (1980), 249-255.
255. Lounsbury, Floyd G. Maya Numeration, Computation, and Calendrical Astronomy. In Dictionary Of Scientific Biography. New York, New York. Charles Scribner's Sons. Volume 15, Supplement 1. 1978. P. 759-818.
256. Visual explanation of a binary clock. Alexander Jones & Eric Pierce. 14 October 2006.
257. David Esparza Hidalgo, Nepohualtzintzin. Computador Prehispanico en Vigencia [The Nepohualtzintzin: a pre-Hispanic computer in use] (Mexico City, Mexico: Editorial Diana, 1977).
258. Bancroft, Hubert Howe (1882). "The Native Races, Volume 2, Civilized Nations. The works of Hubert Howe Bancroft", Volume 2. 1832-1918.
259. "The Maya Mathematical System." Authentic Maya. 2005.
260. Hooker, Richard. "Native American Creation Stories". Washington State University.
261. Walker, Amélie A. "My Trip to Xibalba and Back". Archaeological Institute of America. June 2000.
262. Mizrach, Steve. "The Mayan Sacbe System Analyzed as an Information Web". Florida International University.
263. Dennis Tedlock. "Popol Vuh: The Mayan Book of the Dawn of Life." 1996.
264. "It is believed that there is a supermassive black hole at the Galactic Center of the Milky Way." Credit: ESO. "Mysterious Flares Emitting From Sagittarius A." 9 February, 2012.
265. Lynn V. Foster. "Handbook to Life in the Ancient Maya World." July 7, 2005.
266. Photos of Maya men in traditional costume and figurine. Southwest Missouri State University. John Chuchiak. 2013.
267. "Popol Vuh : The Mayan Book of the Dawn of Life." Dennis Tedlock (Translator) 1996. edited by Jeeni Criscenzo 1997.
268. Justin Kerr. "Enchantment in Mesoamerica." Wall Street Journal. Dow Jones and Company, Inc.. Mar 26, 2011.
269. "The Pleiades, also known as the Seven Sisters" ESO/S. Brunier. eso.org. Photograph: b11. 3 December 2009.
270. Photograph of Stela C, Quirigua. Source: latinamericanstudies.org.
271. "The Sacred Tree of the Ancient Maya." Allen J. Christenson. Journal of Book of Mormon Studies: Volume - 6, Issue - 1, Pages: 1–23 Provo, Utah: Maxwell Institute, 1997.

272. Calabash tree, *Crescentia cujete*. Also known as: higuera tree. Description: This evergreen tropical tree grows up to 10 meters. It has rough bark, simple leaves, and greenish-yellow cauliflorous flowers. Its large spherical fruits have a hard green woody shell. Source: The Natural History Museum. 2013.
273. Friedel, David and Linda Schele, A Forest of Kings: the Untold Story of the Ancient Maya, Harper Perennial 1992.
274. Clare Green. "Pok ta Pok; The Mayan Ball Game. Athletes or Worshipers?" Chichen Itza. Jul 15, 2009.
275. The ball in front of the goal during a game of pok-ta-pok. Photo by Sputnik. Wikipedia. 14 May 2006.
276. Mary Miller. "Extreme Makeover: How painted bodies, flattened foreheads, and filed teeth made the Maya beautiful." Archaeology Magazine, Volume 62 Number 1, January/February 2009.
277. Photo Courtesy: Vera Tiesler/Dirección de Antropología Física. Archaeology Magazine, Volume 62 Number 1, January/February 2009.
278. Photo Courtesy: Vera Tiesler. Archaeology Magazine, Volume 62 Number 1, January/February 2009.
279. Site at Ceibal dating to around 1000 BC. Photo Credit: Takeshi Inomata. "Maya Civilization More Ancient Than Previously Thought." Archaeology Magazine. April 26, 2013.
280. Kukulkan at its finest during the spring equinox. Chichen Itza equinox March 2009. The famous decent of the snake at the temple. Wikipedia. 21 March 2009.
281. Foster, Lynn V. "Handbook to Life in the Ancient Mayan World." New York: Facts on File. 2002.
282. Schele, Linda, and David Freidel. "A Forest of Kings: The Untold Story of the Ancient Maya." New York: Harper Perennial. 1990.
283. Terry Rugeley, "Yucatan's Maya Peasantry and the Origins of the Caste War." San Antonio. 1996.
284. Jacinto Pac to Edward Rhys and John Kingdom, 18 February 1848 in Terry Rugeley, ed. and trans. Maya Wars: Ethnographic Accounts from Nineteenth Century Yucatan, (Norman, 2001).
285. Cecilio Chi to John Fancourt, 23 April 1849, in Rugeley, Maya

Wars.
286. Diorama made by the team at Te Mahi of Aztec chinampas at the Museum of New Zealand Te Papa Tongarewa.

www.ingramcontent.com/pod-product-compliance
Lightning Source LLC
Chambersburg PA
CBHW070105120526
44588CB00032B/920